# VOYAGE

## A Quest for God within
## Orthodox Christian Tradition

by

Lynette A. Smith

ISBN 978-1-928653-39-4

Regina Orthodox Press
PO Box 5288
Salisbury MA 01952

reginaorthodoxpress.com

To all who are on the quest for God

For Dennis

# TABLE OF CONTENTS

# INTRODUCTION

I come from the perspective that life is a voyage, an outward and inward venture toward some sort of discovery. However, if you would have asked me fifteen or so years ago what I believed the nature of my voyage was, I would have given you a different picture of it than if you asked me now.

I was the last of five children born to small town pastors, and from the womb, people of Christian faith surrounded me. Early in life I awakened to a desire for God. At nearly five, I wanted to know how to be good and learned that Jesus, Goodness himself, wanted to dwell in my heart. As I grew, from time to time a restlessness I could not name would stir up inside. My faith tradition, the Assemblies of God, readily acknowledged that conversion to Christ was the beginning, and not the goal, to receiving the many spiritual gifts God wanted to impart. I was taught that my restlessness, then, was naturally a desire for more of God. The theological "distinctive" of the Pentecostal denomination asserted that I could satisfy much of this longing by receiving a "baptism in the Holy Spirit" with speaking in tongues, and the experience would "make one's life and ministry even more effective."[i] Although to my memory, it was not commonly preached in church, my parents in private impressed on me that baptism in the Spirit meant, not an end in itself, but a launching point for allowing God to form me into Christ's image.[ii] At age twelve, during a church youth camp, I experienced what was identified as this baptism.

Even with a godly upbringing, my inner disquiet did not cease. I came to interpret it as stemming from the fact that from ages ten to eighteen, my parents and I lived on the Navajo Reservation where they worked in the public school system. At church and school, I was noticeably in the minority. No matter what friends I made—and they are very dear to me—I believed myself to be an interloper in a culture interwoven with the ways of the clan. When it was time to leave the nest, I reentered the "white man's world," attended a college of my denomination, and ate up all the biblical studies courses with gusto. After graduation I became involved in religious work in my local church and in missions to Southeast Asia. I believed that such a commitment would not only be valuable service, but would also help bring me closer to God and others. It would bring spiritual peace.

How disappointed I was to find that I continued to feel like an ill-at-ease outsider, searching for that yet unnamable thing. In my late twenties, I assumed that I was simply a misfit in this particular expression of Christianity, so over several years I attended parishes of various Protestant-Evangelical denominations. Although the experience broadened my appreciation for the variety of ways God can reveal his grace to people, once more the change of environment did little to assuage my sense of longing.

It became easier to stay to myself, keep the organized church at arm's length, and refuse to become involved beyond attending Sunday morning services a couple of times a month. My attitude went something like this. Being a misfit and an introvert, I may as well seek for more of God on my own. After all, I already know how to pray, I know the basic doctrines and have trained to study and meditate on the Scriptures. I will worship God within my own comfort zone. As a lover of books and the Book, I can read my way toward formation into Christ's image. I will choose a route less clogged with others trying to lumber their way into the kingdom of heaven.

I gave it a try for several years, but it did not work very well. Even an introvert eventually gets lonely trying to worship by herself, especially if that worship is in the context of avoiding the complexity of interacting with people. It would be some time later before I started to accept that I could be both a meditative recluse and one who lives and worships alongside others. At that time, however, I had little inkling of the harmony possible between solitude and fellowship.

When a close friend joined the Orthodox Church, and shortly thereafter a relative showed me a book on Orthodoxy, I decided to look into it. The first time I experienced the Divine Liturgy, my intuition whispered, "Here is something you can really sink your teeth into." It was not long before I discovered the richness that awaited me in Orthodoxy. Part of what I discovered was that the Orthodox Church makes an audacious assertion. She claims to preserve "Holy Tradition," a dynamic continuity of teachings, leadership, and liturgy from the Church's inception in the days of the Apostles until now. That unnamable something I had felt for most of my life yearned toward this ancient yet modern treasure and compelled me to embark on its exploration. Here, if it could be believed, I might at last find my spiritual heritage and stop being a misfit in the Body of Christ. Little wonder then, that when I joined the Orthodox Church, I hoped to stop my perennial struggle and to know where I belonged.

Instead, after a lovely honeymoon period lasting several years, my old conflict came back with a vengeance. I had to face again the paradoxical fact that the Church is indeed God's "holy people" in which the "Holy Spirit" dwells, but we are also fallen people—a mix of good and not so good. The Church is an extremely complicated organism. I know from personal experience that her constituents can perform astonishing acts of sacrificial love and grace and yet perpetrate ways to hurt, marginalize, or overpower members of her own body. It is a truism to say that the Church is not yet perfected, but I have taken a long time even to begin to tolerate this imperfection with more mercy than criticism. Thus, once more, as I had so many occasions in the past, I asked myself, "Do I belong here?" Although reluctant, this time I let up my resistance and admitted, yes, there is a place for people like me in the Church. What made the difference in my response? At least three key factors prepared me to choose to stay on board; in fact, they continue to incite courage for the journey.

One, for the first time in my life, I have a spiritual father confessor to whom I can bear my soul. He puts up with having to listen repeatedly to my struggle, and with empathy and persistence he reflects back to me the balance of life as a Christian pilgrim. A particular lesson of his on embracing the journey just as it is, stands out to me. One summer morning while we were sitting out on his deck, he said to me, "Conflict and struggle in the Church are normal. It is the journey here." I replied, "So if I must live in this conflict and struggle, where does peace enter into it?" "Peace," he said, "is being here now, just sitting, and listening to the birds." To get where I am going, I must be where I am.

Two, the Orthodox saying, "we are lost alone but are saved together" has gotten under my skin. Initially, I did not like this idea much. Isn't it true that if I were the only person on earth, Jesus in his love would have still come to save me? Yes, it is true. However, it is also true that I am not the only person on earth. Much in Scripture points me to the exquisite linkage between God, others, and myself; Orthodox theology also honors both the value of personhood and the splendor of the interdependent design of Christ's Body. Like an organ in a body, it is important that I keep my uniqueness, but equally important that I function within the context of the whole organism. Thus, staying isolated blocks me from moving forward in my quest for Christlikeness and for the spiritual treasures Christ bestows. Nor does isolation help anybody else.

Three, the more I experience the Eucharistic liturgy of the Church, the more I sense that I am becoming rooted in and connected with that which is beyond myself. People within a parish may have all sorts of problems, personal or interpersonal, but when the action and words of the Divine Liturgy take place, something mystically transcendent happens. Even when my body hurts or my mind is too distracted to participate fully, the movement of the Liturgy sustains and carries me forward—if only for short moments. Forward where? Orthodox liturgist Fr. Alexander Schmemman wrote, "The liturgy of the Eucharist is...the journey of the Church into the dimension of the Kingdom...our sacramental entrance into the risen life of Christ."[iii] My experience, limited as it is, resonates with these words.

You may have noticed that I have used the word "journey" several times, and this of course, goes along with my start-off sentence that life is like a voyage. The analogy of voyage to life is ancient, harkening back at least to Homer's 9th century BC *Odyssey*. Several centuries later, early Christians tied the story of Noah and the ark to a sense of the Church's voyage on earth. They understood that in part, the Hebrew Bible (or Old Testament) functioned like a pointer toward the coming person and work of Christ. Tucked throughout Noah's story, they saw foreshadowings, or messages, concerning future realities of Jesus. One interpretation was that the ark was a type of the Body of Christ, the Church.[iv] As the wooden ark provided safety from destructive flood waters for those who went aboard, so the Church is a place of refuge because its pilot, Jesus, through the wood of a cross, provides salvation from sin and death for all who believe on him. Further, the ark, on its transitory adventure, is a figure, or symbol, of the Church "sojourning in this world."[v]

I like these analogies. Through their lens, I can look back in history up to the present and see that sometimes the Holy Ark of the Church moves through tranquil waters, while other times she violently rocks because of dissention within or persecution without. Always the Church manages to sail on without the world's evil pulling her under. She has embarked, not just on a year's meander as Noah's boat did, but on a journey of odyssean proportions. As long as she remains on earth, the Church is in the arduous, yet glorious process of being actualized as the Body of Christ. Because I am part of this Body, I am learning to own the process for myself as well. As one of her passengers, I take the ride much better when I do not kid myself into thinking that the Church should be a vacation cruise ship.

Similar to the passengers of the ark that Noah built, I journey in a vessel that sometimes smells like frankincense, sometimes like a barn. It is certain that I have contributed to both aromas. Yet, like Noah's craft, God has well outfitted the Ark of the Church for navigation through treacherous waters. She has a vast holding of treasure and tools for the journey: sacred Scriptures, liturgy, art, music, examples of holy Saints, and guidance from wise elders. With all this talk of voyages and vessels, just where is the Church bound? We are unabashedly journeying toward perfect communion with God, a union that we will only fully realize in the world to come. Meanwhile, during the voyage of this present life, I, as do countless others, seek to follow the way of Christ so that I may draw ever closer to that union.

As it has many times from my youth and up, my soul still often wrenches with longing for the Ineffable. The difference is I now tend to conduct my quest in the milieu of Orthodox Tradition. This ethos enables me to put my struggle and yearning into words that seem to touch closest to my core. And when words fail, which they inevitably do, I find support in Orthodoxy's encouragement that I engage in silent worship and prayer from the heart.

This book reflects my learning to use the tools and treasures of the Orthodox Tradition as I seek to live my everyday life in the presence of God. While not everything I write or quote points directly to a person, stated canon, or practice of the Orthodox Church, I attempt to express my ponderings within the spirit of Orthodoxy. As I make my way toward discovering the depths and riches of the wisdom and knowledge of God, I hope in these words to pass along some portion of the treasure I have garnered.[vi]

Using the analogy of life as a voyage, I group the book into six aspects of a sea expedition. *What I've Been Looking For* carries the idea that I am on a journey not just to wander aimlessly, but with hope of a discovery and a destination. *Sick at Sea* brings out ways in which I strive to find my "sea legs," or spiritual balance, and recover from dis-ease of mind. *No Solo Voyage* emphasizes that I take my life's journey in the company not only of God, but also of others, including angels, saints who have died before me, and earth's creatures, too. Sometimes I must cope with being seemingly off-course, *Land-locked* in a spiritual desert, and allow the experience to enfold and teach me as a normal part of my quest. The quest for God is in fact a most daring route, for *Dying to Live* reveals that I will only fully live out the journey when I take the risk of dying, surrendering myself to Christ's venture. *Are We There Yet?* examines my God-given limitations to evaluate progress toward spiritual maturity, my need to find rest in a swirling world, and to receive the Saints' encouragement to persevere until the journey is complete.

# ACKNOWLEDGMENTS

I owe much of the content of this book to innumerable people and experiences God has allowed me to encounter throughout my life. I am especially grateful to my parents (may they rest in peace) for bringing me up in the love of Christ. Appreciation goes to my family, friends, pastors, and professors who have aided my development along the way.

Thanks to Mother Nina and Ken Munger for piquing my interest in the Orthodox way. Special gratitude to Fr. Les Bundy, who fathers me in the Faith and provides untiring spiritual guidance. I am indebted to his editorial advice throughout this book's evolution. To my fellow parishioners at St. Columba Orthodox Church for their friendship and communion. To Carol Toensing who gave me the initial encouragement to create this work. My gratitude to Frank Schaeffer at Regina Orthodox Press for inviting me to submit the manuscript. To Gean Munger, who proofread the final draft.

Highest thanks belongs to my husband, Dennis. Without his deep commitment and support I could have never completed this project.

# AUTHOR'S NOTE

For those readers who attend Eastern Rite Orthodox parishes and may not recognize some of the liturgical references in this book, I attend a Western Rite Orthodox parish, under the jurisdiction of the Antiochian Orthodox Christian Archdiocese in America. We use the rite of St. Tikhon. Although the wording is not identical to St. Chrysostom's rite, both celebrations contain the same basic elements. The Archdiocese confirms, "Orthodox people of both Rites worship together. The clergy are interchangeable, they share the same hierarchy and the spiritual unity of the faith."[vii]

Some readers may recognize my liturgical quotes are similar to the Anglican Book of Common Prayer. The rite of St. Tikhon is an Orthodox adaptation of the worship rites that the early Church in Rome carried to Scotland, Ireland, and England. It is also similar to the Rite of St. Gregory the Great.

i "Beliefs of the Assemblies of God."
http://www.ag.org/top/beliefs/gendoct_02_baptismhs.cfm.

ii Ibid. From a stated doctrinal standpoint, the Assemblies of God is concerned "that some Pentecostals look on the Baptism and tongues as ends in themselves rather than as means to a much greater end. The Baptism is the entry experience introducing the believer to the beauty and power of the Spirit-filled life."

iii Alexander Schmemann, *For the Life of the World,* (Crestwood, N.Y.: St. Vladimir's Seminary Press, 1972), 26.

iv C.f., Ephraim the Syrian "Hymn I" *Nineteen Hymns on the Nativity;* Cyprian of Carthage *Epistle 74:15;* St. Augustine of Hippo *On the Catechising of the Uninstructed* 27:53; Gregory Thaumaturgos *Fourth Homily;* Melito the Philosopher "Discourse IV" *On Faith.* All in *The Early Church Fathers, Edinburg Edition* [CD-ROM] (Gervais, O.R.: Harmony Media, 1995-2006).

v Augustine of Hippo *City of God*, 15:26.

vi Rom. 11:33.

vii Antiochian Orthodox Christian Archdiocese of North America, "Western Rite: A Brief Introduction," http://www.antiochian.org/node/22395.

# WHAT I'VE BEEN LOOKING FOR

A longing—primal and nearly wordless—that I felt as a young person still stirs me decades later. I believe that the yearning has everything to do with God. So I embark on a voyage of spiritual exploration, hopefully not in aimless wandering, but in hope of a discovery and a destination. Yet what am I looking for and how will I know when I have found "it"?

Jesus, in one of his well-known teachings, promises the spiritual explorer,

> "Ask, and it will be given to you; seek, and you will find; knock, and the door will be opened to you…Enter by the narrow gate; for wide is the gate and broad is the way that leads to destruction, and there are many who go in by it. Because narrow is the gate and difficult is the way which leads to life, and there are few who find it."[1]

My yearning may have everything to do with God, but since I live in an environment of the "world, flesh, and devil" I face the temptation to lower my sights and choose, what on the surface, seem to be wider, more attractive and immediate gates to spirituality. What God gives in answer to my request may not appear in a neat package, pre-programmed, or easily comprehensible; rather, his gifts may come wrapped up in paradox, hidden behind nature, or slipped into works of art. Most absurd of all, God in his strange love has placed his Kingdom not only among humanity in general, but also within my unfathomable and fractured heart. Mystically, my quest for God means that I travel beyond myself, and yet become more myself in the process.

# Glory Bypassed

*Original sin was not just an erroneous choice…but rather a refusal to ascend toward God.*[2]

Fr. Georges Florovsky

"The devil took him to a very high mountain and showed him all the kingdoms of the world and their splendor," St. Matthew says of one temptation Jesus faced. As a carpenter turned itinerant teacher, Jesus' simple life was unworthy of the status he should have if he was the legitimate "son of God." Absolute power and wealth could be his for a little bend of the knee in the devil's direction. Jesus turned down the devil's offer, not only because it was an evil being who offered him all the kingdoms, but also because the proposition amounted to nothing whatsoever in the end.

It is easy to think that the so-called "world, flesh, and devil" are able to turn my head because they offer such a profusion of pleasurable options. However, society is filled with selfishness, hatred, violence, betrayal, lust, envy, arrogance, and the like, not because it wants too much, but because it wants too little. It wants everything but God, who ironically, is all in all. I am irritated with our human archetypes, Adam and Eve, because they bartered away the best of all possible arrangements for a panacea they did not need. What is more irritating is that I am just as easy of a sell. I know better than to equate the promise of eternal life and all its attending benefits with anything currently offered on earth, and yet continue to lower my sights, headed to that same branch from which Eve picked her fruit.

Down here in the long rows of choices, I cannot even linger for the turning of the leaves. Somehow, I do not want to bring desire to browse. I am hungry, but not insatiable nearly enough to amass the opulent far flung colors, textures, aromas, and flavors. Mist and stream whisper at my feet, "All are yours: the world, or life, or death, or things present, or things to come; all are yours."[3] Despite its sumptuousness, that divine 'all' is too immense to see and too much to grasp in the hand. All may as well be nothing.

What is this attraction away from the lavish toward a single obsession? One conspicuous fruit of one conspicuous tree, I want your virtuous and wicked wink to lock my eyes. I want to press my fingertips into your skin, pull you away from all the others to my mouth. I will gorge on the knowing, until the probity in you pierces all the more for its seduction, and the evil in you lulls my dignity into a stupor. If it will take me straight to the heights, then go ahead, fling me down into the flames of nihilist bravado. I don't care; give me my kingdom, my power, my glory. Now.

The tree that I am free to eat from stands rooted there where it has always been. Its boughs loaded with immortality, beckon me to the stars. Neighboring trunks wave their arms all around me, wafting joy to beast and butterfly. Why then do I look the other way to the tree here—the only one whose fruit I should not eat? That one I stare at, while the many trees, all of them free to me, I pass by. Acres of God's orchards invite me to feast long and gradually train my palate for splendor. They promise that I will find what I am looking for. Step by step, I would ascend Eden's summit, preparing for wisdom beyond sentience, and there the Transfigured

would feed me the (once forbidden) delicacy of the
Saints.

Lynette A. Smith

# Footsteps in the Sea

*"Your way was in the sea, Your path in the great waters, and Your footsteps were not known. You led your people like a flock by the hand of Moses and Aaron."*[4]

Asaph the Poet

God's normal path tends to go through places or situations I cannot necessarily follow easily. When he led the Israelites out of Egypt, his path put them right in front of an obstacle they did not have means to overcome. He, of course, in anthropomorphic terms, slopped right through the Red Sea because it was nothing to him. The Israelites could not see his path because it was covered by water that he had not yet moved out of the way for them.[5]

It was the same in the desert a few days later. The Children of Israel doubted, "Can God make a way in the wilderness?"[6] Apparently, he can. God's usual path is just as liable to be right through bleak, bewildering desolation and danger as it is through intense beauty, delight, and joy. Any one of those courses can be more than a human can cope with on her own. Why?

One reason is simply the vast difference between God and me. His holiness and glory is such that his very Being automatically overwhelms what he creates. I can experience this kind of proportional majesty in my own back yard. I step on an ant nearly every summer day, not so much because I am trying to squash it or am angry at it, but because I am so great in size compared with an ant. My path just naturally marches through its little world. What are huge undertakings for it—to collect food,

7

dispose of waste, and build a home—are not even within my typical notice.

Likewise, my purposes and endeavors are unfathomable and undoable for the ant. If it were not for God's mercy and love for his creation, the simple act of his coming through would destroy everything in his path. Unless I am an arachnologist, I am not going to spend much time with ants, and even an arachnologist cannot truly experience the ant's life. However, God gave his Son to actually become a human being and dwell right down here with us. Accessible, less intimidating, utterly empathetic.

Another reason I may not cope well with God's way for me is that I tend to underestimate the glorious destination he has in mind. I reconstitute his value system into what I think is a shorter and more immediate path of gratification. This is a common and long-standing problem. Ancient Scripture teaches that from the time of the creation of the universe and planet earth, God designed us human beings to be made in his image, to become perfect as he is perfect, and be progressively filled with all his fullness.[7] To start with, he set the man and woman in Eden, a paradise with the full potential of perfect divine-human communion. However, instead of continuing to opt for God's will they chose to settle for much less. They believed that the fruit of one of God's creations—instead of God himself—would quickly do the job of satisfying their desire to be filled, to know all things, to be like God.[8] It didn't, and it still doesn't. We have been wandering the globe and cosmos trying to recapture this reality ever since.

God, however, is utterly devoted to helping me recapture the reality. The Greek elders of Christianity had a word for it: *theosis*. It means the process of a human becoming totally filled with God. English theologians translate the word as divinization, or deification, scary words for a lot of believers. However dangerously heretical it may sound initially, the Orthodox Church is unafraid to declare that theosis is the goal of my faith. She is also careful to explain that theosis does not imply I am actually becoming God in my essence, but that in this life I begin to participate in his divine nature as Adam and Eve were meant to do prior to their fall.[9] Another way of saying it is that step by step I begin to enjoy union with Christ by his grace, until after this earthly life, I experience unity in full measure.[10] This is no more than what Jesus prays for us.[11]

As he called the children of Israel to leave Egypt and go back to Canaan, God calls me to choose his plan and return to paradise, to the kingdom "flowing with milk and honey." He takes me through difficulties, as he did them, to train me to trust him to get me home. Then, once I am on the other side of the test of faith, like Miriam after the Israelites had crossed the Red Sea, I can break out the tambourine and dance a little.[12]

Lynette A. Smith

# Paradox:
# The Name of the Game

*An ancient held up an infant, but the infant upheld the ancient.*[13]

Antiphon, Presentation of Christ

The deeper I submerge myself into this phenomenon called Christianity, the more I encounter paradox. Biblical writers often make statements and tell stories that seem self-contradictory or absurd. Then a bunch of people claim to unravel some part of the riddle found in these words and have the audacity to believe it means something infinitely important. According to them, the apparent contradictions and absurdities express viable truth. Whether or not this is fully the case, at least these riddles are potential mediums through which truth reaches into human experience. Paradox.

As a participant in the cycle of the Church year, I notice that paradox shows up frequently in the liturgy of major feast days. Take the old man, Simeon, for example, a key player in the Presentation of Jesus at the Temple celebrated just after each New Year.[14] God gives Simeon a close connection with his Holy Spirit, who lets him know that he will not die before he has seen the Lord's Messiah. St. Simeon waits and waits, hanging on.

One morning, the Spirit propels him to go to the Temple in Jerusalem. At the same time, parents are bringing their infants to present them to the Lord. Simeon makes a beeline for a particular family, namely that of Joseph and Mary, and takes the tiny Jesus into his arms.

"Here he is at last!" declares Simeon, "The consolation of Israel and salvation to the Gentiles." What a huge order for a small package! Simeon is not only making a prediction, but also stating present reality. St. Augustine of Canterbury expresses it well, "The ancient Simeon bore in his arms the new-born Christ, and all the while, Christ ruled and upheld the old man."[15] He holds what is a very little child on the outside, but on the inside of that child are held Simeon and by proxy, Jews, Gentiles, and all of creation. This marvel marks the ultimate paradox of Christianity. Through the Incarnation, the Son of God empties himself so that he may sustain all things.[16]

While musing on Jesus' presentation at the Temple and all that led up to that day, St. Ambrose in one of his sermons observes that God does not leave any gender, class, or human condition out of the possibility of being in the middle of life-giving paradox.[17] Perhaps that is why St. Luke in the opening chapters of his Gospel takes pains to include an extraordinary mix of people and creatures who are present for the events surrounding Christ's birth.

A sterile woman bears;<br>
an archangel announces;<br>
a young virgin conceives;<br>
an unborn child leaps for joy;<br>
a doubting mute declares;<br>
a carpenter sees visions;<br>
a king is born in a cave;<br>
a beast gives up her manger;<br>
heavenly hosts sing;<br>
sheep and herders are the first to know;<br>
an anchorite widow prophesies;<br>
and an old man finds what he's been looking for.

A part of me wants genuine Christianity to be orderly. I want the Lord to allow only the most consistent of its practitioners to be in charge of its ministry and for the rest of the followers to have most of their ducks in a row. Presumably then I would have an easier time of becoming a better Christian myself. After a few decades of fruitlessly hoping for this kind of Christianity and being perennially disappointed, I suspect it is time to let go. If I am to discover the true existence that I seek, I really do not have a choice. To anyone, and through anyone, whether I like it or not, God can show truth that leads to the redemptive Way.

"Go ahead, Lynette," Simon and all the cloud of St. Luke's witnesses whisper, "plunge into the paradox."

Lynette A. Smith

# Illustrators
# of the Holy Beautiful

I was flipping through Bernard Meehan's introduction to *The Book of Kells* the other day.[18] Actually, I could not "flip" through a book of this sort. The highly vibrant and decorative pages of this ancient Celtic Gospel manuscript made me want to slow down for a longer look. *The Book of Kells*, as Meehan aptly describes it, "is the most lavishly decorated of a series of gospel manuscripts produced between the seventh and ninth centuries, when Irish art and culture flourished at home and in centres of Irish missionary activity overseas."[19] It is a prime example of Orthodoxy expressing itself through a western culture before the Great Schism divided Eastern and Western Christianity around 1054 AD.

The book's illuminators made constant use of the famous Irish knot, a symbol of eternalness. With this and numerous other finely detailed motifs, they drew exquisite borders around icons of the Virgin and Child and symbolic portraits of the Evangelists Matthew, Mark, Luke, and John. They also decorated initials, important words, and phrases. The illuminators did not just sit down and dash out these illustrations freehand. Instead, they composed the drawings with complex mathematical formula that required knowing their way around compasses, dividers, set-squares, rulers, and French curve templates.

The longer I sat and looked at these lovely pages, the more the constant, almost wild, movement created by the knots, curling vines, dots, and circular crosses drew me in. I felt the power of the interplay between these curves and circles. They seemed to illustrate the continuous movement of the Lord God as he set about to create the splendor of the heavens and earth. I caught a glimpse of a God who is always reaching into his world to bring forth his splendor, and my heart beat a little faster for a moment. Possibly I had come in contact with the Holy Beautiful.

In an article on the subject, Orthodox theologian, Fr. John Breck, affirms my experience of God's action through beauty. He quotes St. Maximus the Confessor: "The divine…is subject to movement; and as that which is intensely longed for and loved; it moves towards itself everything that is receptive of this force and love… since it thirsts to be thirsted for, longs to be longed for, and loves to be loved." [20] The beauty I saw in *The Book of Kells*, then, is one way God declares his longing and love for me. When Orthodox authors write on the subject of beauty, they often quote Dostoevsky's line, "Beauty will save the world." This phrase is broad enough to be interpreted numerous ways, but one way I understand this salvation is that God's beauty, whether bold or subtle, seeks to attract me, and whosoever will, toward his grace. Breck goes on to write, "Beauty actively reaches beyond itself to fill all of creation, and it draws to itself all those who seek it, to transform them into its own splendor." My visceral response to beauty, which often evokes an unspeakable yearning, is nothing less than a normal response to God's longing to take me into his love.

As I continued to study the *Kells* iconography, I gradually became aware that most of the decorative twinings lay within carefully set limits. The limits showed up in the edges of each page's dimensions, in border lines, and rectangular frames. As I gazed at the boundaries that outlined and supported the flowing beauty within them, I connected for a moment with a profound stillness. These Celtic artists had somehow captured a further sense of the Holy Beautiful: the constancy of a God who does not change his character.

The Church Fathers believe that when Moses climbed up through the clouds to meet with God on Mt. Sinai his face shone because he participated in Divine Beauty.[21] Father Vladimir Berzonsky comments that Moses was placed "in the atmosphere of silence, stillness and the foretaste of eternity."[22] He applies Moses' experience to life today, "To speak with God in prayer, one must shut down the noise of the world, turn off the concerns that whirl around in the mind, and imbibe the nourishment of the soul. *Here is the heart's longing—the voice of silence in the presence of the holy.*"[23]

Psalm 96 has a lovely line, "O worship the LORD in the beauty of holiness."[24] I have often wondered what this kind of worship looks like. The beauty of God is everywhere: in the shimmering green neck of a mallard, the striking lines of the Hamilton Building at the Denver Museum of Art, the beaming smile of a child with Down's syndrome, the iconography of the Orthodox Church of which *The Book of Kells* is a part. When I absorb beauty, I can take the occasion to lift my inexpressible longing for love to God. I can choose to accept his love in return and worship, not the created things, but God, Holy Beauty himself.

Holy Beauty began the world, infusing it with loveliness that I still enjoy today, although it exists within ugliness and manifold imperfections. Nevertheless, to see beauty now is to catch a foretaste of the pure brilliance I will behold when God completely manifests the Kingdom of heaven at the *parousia,* the coming of Christ.

> One thing I have desired of the LORD,
> that will I seek:
> that I may dwell in the house of the LORD
> all the days of my life,
> to behold the beauty of the LORD,
> and to inquire in His temple.[25]

# Where is the Kingdom of God?

*When He was asked by the Pharisees when the kingdom of God*
*would come, He answered them and said, "The Kingdom of God*
*does not come with observation; nor will they say, 'See here!' or 'See*
*there!' For indeed, the Kingdom of God is within you.*[26]

Luke the Evangelist

All my life I have heard Jesus' parables about the
Kingdom of God, but no matter how many times I hear
or read his descriptions and explanations, the Kingdom
remains elusive. Maybe this is because I am like the
Pharisees who ask Jesus when the Kingdom of God
would come. Theirs is not only a question of timing, but
also how they will know that the Kingdom of God had
actually arrived. They and I both suspect that God's
Kingdom does not seem to be around yet, or we would
see better evidence of it, wouldn't we? The violent forces
of nature, not to speak of the brokenness of sin, scar the
beauty of creation and disrupt the harmony we expect in
a kingdom God would build.

In answer to the Pharisees, Jesus says that they cannot
discover God's Kingdom by the five senses alone but that
it requires dropping into an alternate universe. He states
what methods will not work and where the Kingdom will
not be located; only at the end of his answer does Jesus
tell the Pharisees where the Kingdom can be found. The
Kingdom contains more than the usual kinds of
observable data that humans can manipulate, and careful
observation is precisely the Pharisees' habit when they are
around Jesus. They would have made good scientists.

Still, even as far as natural science has advanced today, no one can collect DNA, categorize genomes, synthesize formulae, and find conclusive evidence for the existence of God's Kingdom. Jesus affirms in the Gospels how ineffective people are to try to identify the Kingdom of God by conventional means. He does this simply by using analogies or parables when talking about it. It is true that he employs observable objects and situations—a mustard seed, soil samples, a king settling accounts, a farmer sowing—but he extracts a deeper, and often unexpected, significance from them.

A highly expensive pearl is one of Jesus' choices for a parable on the Kingdom that piques my curiosity:

> The Kingdom of heaven is like a merchant seeking beautiful pearls, who, when he found one pearl of great price, went and sold all that he had and bought it.[27]

I do not own any costly pearls, but when I pop into the jewelry store to have my wedding ring cleaned, I see some lovely specimens, so I can nod my head at Jesus' parable and say, "Yes, I get the part that this particular pearl was worth a lot of money." However, to understand the Kingdom of God as pearl-esque, I have to look more closely for implications beyond Jesus' pearl being extraordinarily nice and very expensive.

For one thing, the rationality of the merchant seems suspect. Why would he liquidate all his assets for this gem? Although I may be somewhat of a rarity among women, I could look at high-end pearls all day long and not be tempted to buy one strand. How is the merchant going to use this thing now that it is all he has in the bank? How is he going to feed himself and his family with it, for goodness' sake?

Obviously the parable bothers me, and I suspect Jesus meant for it to. Long after I have lost interest in pearls, I am still seeking to understand the passion of that crazy merchant. What is it about the Kingdom of God that would make me realize that it is what I have been looking for all my life? Where is this realm in which all needs are met, yet I can be persuaded to first let go of everything else? The fourth century poet, St. Ephraim the Syrian, expressed a similar wonder in the message of the pearl with which I find resonance:

> On a certain day a pearl did I take up, my brethren;
> I saw in it mysteries pertaining to the Kingdom;
> semblances and types of the Majesty;
> it became a fountain,
> and I drank out of it mysteries of the Son.[28]

Lynette A. Smith

# Inward Expedition

*Find the door to the inner chamber of your soul, and you will discover the door to the Kingdom of Heaven.*[29]

St. John Chrysostom

What a relief it was for an introspective like me to learn Orthodox elders teach that getting to know myself is essential to my pilgrimage. I had been doing self-analysis for years, and now I actually have ecclesial permission to continue! That is, to a degree. Some types of self-analysis are limited in their effectiveness and end goal, even leading to self-absorption. Nevertheless, to enter into the fullness of the Kingdom, my journey must take both an upward and inward movement. St. Paul likens his journey to a marathon track winding its way to the mountain peaks "for the prize of the *upward* call of God."[30] Jesus says as he finishes his discourse on where the kingdom of God resides, "For indeed, the Kingdom of God is *within* you."[31]

At thirteen, I was very ready to explore what made me tick. By nineteen I found college 101 psychology and sociology classes fascinating. Something in the back of my mind suspected the interest in these subjects lay beyond acquiring mere knowledge. Sure enough, at twenty-six I began a multi-year stint on a Christian psychologist's couch, suffering chronic depression and confused over my identity in the church and world. My coping methods, broken as they were, kept me functional while my mind and spirit whirled in chaos.

Psychoanalysis helped fit many puzzle pieces together about my experiences and corresponding reactions to them. Therapy also gave me a safe venue to begin the process of grieving, forgiveness, and reconciliation over past hurts. However, long before I was sufficiently well and had worked out whether I could or should carry out a missionary vocation, I applied to my denomination's mission's agency. A year and a half later Continental Airlines flew me ten thousand miles to Thailand. Four months after arriving in the country, I was taking my meals in a mental hospital in Denver, Colorado. I had been just days away from jumping off the balcony of my ninth floor Bangkok apartment.

I was relieved not to continue a mission vocation, yet carried an enormous sense of having failed God, my supporters, the mission agency, and myself. I wished to know that God and others loved and accepted me, not only for what I could do for the cause of Christ, but just for me. Yet, who was "me"? After I peeled away the tentacled layer called "trying to measure up," all I seemed to see were more layers marked "dropout in the ministry" "needy," "depressed," "hypocrite," "disobedient." Did a Self exist down there who was more than the sum of her infirmities and iniquities?

I knew that Christian theology affirmed this inner person indeed existed and should grow within the structure of God's will. However, if I had encountered St. Chrysostom's above quote at this stage, I would have asked, "How am I ever to find the door of my inner heart?" My psychotherapists said my shattered self needed to reintegrate and acquire healthy esteem. I agreed to a certain extent, yet could scarcely identify which self I was supposed to integrate and esteem. The arguments in my head, added to outside influences over what I should do, whom I should relate to, and ultimately, whom I should be, raised a disorienting cacophony. As Walker Percy described the state of all humanity, I was "lost in the cosmos."[32] What would it take to be found? The tools I typically used to approach the self—over protection, morbid loathing, and over indulgence—simply worked against each other.

Of all the good things I longed for during those dark years, one wild idea clung to the edges of my sanity. I wanted my genuine self—whoever she was—to enshrine the genuine presence of God, and from that center, find a way to thrive rather than merely survive. Ironically, the only way I could have desired such impossibility came from the very presence of God already working in the same self whom I understood so little. From down in those depths came a dogged pursuit for wellbeing, and through a variety of spiritual and mental health caregivers who continued what psychotherapy began, the mending process finally took hold.

One unexpected avenue of renewal has come from the writings of holy sages in the Orthodox Church. What they teach and exemplify about knowing the self does not necessarily cover every aspect of the exploration. Yet I am discovering that their insight and advice allows my voyage into the self to take on a new clarity and dimension. As I read the wisdom of the elders, I learn more about the nature of my heart and her challenges. Although these sages do not use the psychological language I am used to, they offer me ways to engage in an increasingly balanced self-analysis. They are the Marco Polos of the heart and graciously pass on their travel knowledge. One such ancient holy man uncannily observes:

Within the heart are unfathomable depths. There are reception rooms and bedchambers..., doors and porches, and many offices and passages. In it is the workshop of righteousness and of wickedness...The heart is but a small vessel: and yet dragons and lions are there, and there poisonous creatures and all the treasures of wickedness; rough, uneven paths are there, and gaping chasms. There likewise is God, there are angels, there life and the Kingdom, there light and the apostles, the heavenly cities and the treasures of grace.[33]

From my youth, a stanza in Psalm 42 has never stopped touching an inner chord. I now understand why. It expresses the yearning for my self to find its meaning in God. I am connecting that yearning with a greater awareness of how fathomless my inner depths are and that Christ has already plumbed those depths. He is in process of cleansing and repairing the fractures, and furthermore, has no reluctance to reside there.

Deep calls to deep at the noise of Your waterfalls;
all Your waves and billows have gone over me.
The LORD will command His loving kindness
in the daytime,
and in the night His song shall be with me—
a prayer to the God of my life.

# SICK AT SEA

When most people climb aboard a vessel and move out to open sea, it is not long before they experience seasickness. Generally, after a few hours or days, their system adapts to the ship's movements in the water and they can dare to walk about the deck, eat, and engage in activity. They have found their "sea legs." Even so, if a strong wind or storm comes up, the passengers may revert to the old stumbling around and nausea until the weather calms.

Likewise, when I embark on the spiritual voyage, I must strive to find my spiritual balance, or "sea legs." Aboard the ark of the Holy Church, I come to Christ needing to see myself as a child of God, yes, but often out of harmony with his ways and thoughts. I require ongoing spiritual healing in the context of my daily experiences, and throughout the passage, my whole being must adjust to the movements of life in the world.

Christian sages counsel that I need to address dis-ease of mind and its thought processes continually. In conjunction with mental regulation, I must undergo a change of heart through repentance and humility. As I persistently implement spiritual disciplines over the months and years, I will cultivate what is hopefully an increasing measure of soundness. At points along the way, however, difficulties arise that bring the process to a standstill, and I must reach out for assistance.

Lynette A. Smith

## Case of the Logismoi Virus

A while back, I came down with writer's block, a common virus that wordsmiths experience. Oh, there was not a lack of thoughts running around in my head; instead, they were the bad bacterial kind. I had several favorite phrases I rehearsed repeatedly, and quite a few sophistries as well, that seemed feverishly to take over my brain, and certainly sapped me of my creative juices.

My problem is a common and an age-old one. I have learned that Desert elders, theologians, and spiritual directors within Orthodox Christian Tradition have been endeavoring to understand and combat these mental viruses for centuries. Characteristic of these students of human nature is how deeply attuned they are to the vagaries of the mind and how to successfully contend with them. The nineteenth century Russian Orthodox saint, Theophan the Recluse, gave this diagnosis to the struggle of his young spiritual daughter, Anastasia:

> Thoughts…are always in the head, chasing one another, and it is not possible to control them…All your inner disorder is due to the dislocation of your powers, the mind and the heart each going their own way. [The head is] a crowded rag market: it is not possible to pray to God there.[34]

Alcoholics Anonymous fittingly calls Theophan's rag market, "stinking thinking." The Greek word that Orthodoxy has historically used for such thoughts is *logismoi*. Technically, logismoi are not always negative thoughts, but since ancient times, this has been the common use of the word. For example, St. Paul personifies logismoi as prosecution and defense going on in one's mind, or as fortresses of false reasoning that need tearing down.[35]

If there are definitions and diagnoses for the invasion of logismoi, there are also remedies that the Orthodox Church recommends. The classic advice comes from another Desert Father, St. John Climacus, who describes three different levels of treatment.

> It is one thing to pray for rescue from bad thoughts, another to stand up against them, and another still to despise and ignore them. The first situation is exemplified by the one who said, "O God, come and help me" (Ps. 69:2); the second by, "I will speak a word of contradiction to those who reproach me" (Ps. 118:42)…And of the third the witness is the psalmist: "The proud have gone too far in breaking the law, but I have not turned aside from my contemplation of You" (Ps. 118:51—St. Climacus' version).[36]

St. Climacus' first level of care is like hurrying to the emergency room when I have sliced my finger open with a paring knife. All thoughts of eating dinner and enjoying a movie abruptly end. So too, when the damaging effects of logismoi have stopped other activities dead cold, and I cannot staunch the hemorrhaging, I had better quit trying and call on God for help. The Apostle Paul expressed it this way, "Be anxious for nothing, but in everything by prayer and supplication, with thanksgiving, let your requests be made known to God."[37]

The second level of mental care is as antibiotics are to a bacterial infection. I take a good look at the little squiggly false thoughts swimming around and combat them with the truth. Abba Moses, a late fourth century Desert Father recommended an intentional focus on excellent things.

> If . . . we constantly return to meditating on Holy Scripture and raise our awareness to the recollection of spiritual realities and to the desire for perfection and the hope of future blessedness, it is inevitable that [these] . . . will cause the mind to *dwell* on that which we have been meditating.[38]

The third level is preventive treatment: do not let the logismoi bugs take over the mind. Yes, they will hang around, like the ever-present cold microorganisms in the back of the throat, but if I build up my spiritual immune system, I might be able to more effectively ward off coming down with the logismoi virus.

How do Orthodox spiritual directors teach me to build up the mental immune system? The most common advice I have found is to apply a principle I think of as "garbage in, garbage out." For most people, the human body is tough; at least in its youth; it puts up with quite a bit of nutritional abuse. By the time I turn forty or fifty, though, if I am still consuming the same amounts of junk food as I was at twenty, my body is going to show the "garbage out" results of "garbage in." My arteries might clog up, straining the heart, or my insulin levels may descend into diabetes.

My mind is not different from my body in this respect; in fact, rubbish seems to affect it more quickly and adversely. If early Christians fled to the desert in part to rid themselves of worldly distractions, how much more glut do their spiritual sons and daughters have to contend with sixteen hundred years later! These days, by the time a person is an adolescent the profusion of data she sees and hears through electronic media jam-packs a mind already cluttered with both the important and utter drivel. By age twenty or thirty, even prior to the era of the internet, I had already accumulated more than enough information to either support or ravage a proper discernment of self, the world, and God. St. Theophan the Recluse advises Anastasia, "Do not give free reign to your senses, especially the eyes and ears. Do not allow them to see everything, hear everything, and be concerned with everything indiscriminately."[39] Abba Moses addresses the harmful effects that mutate from such a slipshod openness to whatever one comes across.

> If we are overcome by laziness and negligence and let ourselves be taken up with wicked behavior and silly conversations, or if we get involved in worldly concerns and unnecessary preoccupations, the result will be as if a kind of weed had sprung up, which will impose harmful labor on our heart.[40]

I appreciate the approach Abba Moses takes when he warns that careless thinking imposes "harmful labor on the heart." He is not focusing on how corrupt or contemptible logismoi are in the eyes of God, although legitimately he might have. Rather, he chooses to appeal to my natural, divinely given self-preservation, almost as if I were a patient with arteriosclerosis who must make life changes to prevent a heart attack.

Thus, with every passing year, if I do not put some sort of mental filter into play, I am going to reduce my ability to concentrate on what really matters. As Theophan warned in my earlier quote, I will increasingly experience a "dislocation" of my powers. My wandering, dissipated mind will not be available to reinforce what my heart knows is choice and pure, and the ability to accomplish God's desire for my life weakens.

Consequently, I will find myself not only coming down with occasional writer's block, but suffer a chronic case of Christ-follower's block.

Lynette A. Smith

# With all Due Disrespect

*It is one thing to pray for rescue from bad thoughts, another to stand up against them, and another still to despise and ignore them.*[41]

St. John Climacus

Besides disciplining myself to be selective with what I allow into my mind, St. John teaches that I should go so far as to despise and ignore bad thoughts. To actually scorn and discount certain thoughts can be quite a challenge if they are habitual logismoi stuck inside my brain. Over the years, I have accumulated mental scripts that play repetitively when and where I am most vulnerable.

> *Those people are stupid idiots!*
> *Prayer takes too much time; I'll handle it myself.*
> *Things are hopeless.*
> *Why bother?*
> *I'm a stupid idiot!*

Negative habitual thoughts can be so embedded in my mental processes that they become mere white noise in the background. Consequently, I trick myself into believing that I am successfully ignoring them, until life's stresses turn the volume up. Then the noise is deafening. Therefore, before I can genuinely disregard internal, insidious thoughts, I first have to stop and pay attention to what they are. I cannot despise what I do not recognize.

What about the bad ideas that are not habitual, but come in from outside myself through media, break room chatter, and elsewhere? I have a tendency to give near-equal opportunity to a number of notions that catch my attention. I mull them over, and even when I wind up disagreeing with them, I expend a lot of mental and emotional energy to reach that conclusion. Even silly little snatches of past conversations or a reminder to remove the clothes out of the dryer can interrupt the most serene time of meditation.

During a conversation with the abbess at St. Barbara's Orthodox Monastery, I brought up my struggle with thoughts bombarding me during prayer. She told me a helpful story that I later remembered reading in Fr. Anthony Coniaris' book, *Philokalia: Bible of Orthodox Spirituality*.

> Two [20th century] pilgrims once asked an ascetic Orthodox monk of Mt. Athos: "To what extent are we responsible for the thoughts that attack our intellect? The Elder replied, "Airplanes pass over where I live. I cannot hinder the airplanes. I'm not responsible for that. I would be responsible if I began to build an airport. The acceptance of the attacks, which is consent, can be compared to the airport."[42]

I realize with chagrin that there are quite a few landing strips in my cranium. I simply take incoming logismoi much more seriously than they deserve. This means I empower those thoughts with the viability to continue to exist in my mind. One time I mentioned the frustration I was having with attacking thoughts to a friend. She motioned her hand over her head as if waving off flies, and said, "Tell them, 'Oh, it's just you again.'" How disarming her advice was.

Laurence, abbot of the Benedictine monastery, Christ in the Desert, says in his commentary on St. Benedict's Rule that "at the heart of this fight with thoughts...is the recognition that I am NOT my thoughts."[43] If I will embrace that key concept, I can begin to detach myself from the bad thoughts I have. I can realize that logismoi are not worth giving the time of day. To disrespect these kinds of thoughts means I am learning to respect who God is making me to be in his purity, faith, and love.

Lynette A. Smith

# Miles and Metanoia[*]

Not quite four years old, my great-nephew, Miles, had yet to learn what the word "lie" meant, but one evening, he got his first lesson. His mom, Alyssa, told him to pick up his Legos® in the living room, put them in their box, and then get ready for bed. In short order, the house became quiet. She called to Miles, "Did you put your Legos® in the box?" "Yes," he answered. On her way up to tuck Miles into bed, she passed by the living room. All his Legos® were still spread over the floor, but the boy was apparently already upstairs.

Alyssa had caught Miles in his first lie. My niece knew she needed to approach this very carefully. Breathing a prayer for help, she entered his room and said, "Miles, Mommy is very sad."

Startled, he asked, "Why are you sad?" Alyssa answered, "Mommy is sad because you lied to her."

"What does that mean?"

"It means that you did not tell me the truth. You told me that you had put away your Legos®, but they are still all over the floor. So Mommy is very sad that you lied to her."

With this, Miles burst into tears, "I'm sorry, Mommy." It wrenched her heart. She let him cry it out, then said, "This time Mommy is going to pick up your Legos® for you. But so you will remember to obey me and to tell me the truth, you cannot play with your Legos® tomorrow. I

---

[*] Permission was granted to use this story.

am going to put them up on a shelf."

The next morning while Alyssa was preparing breakfast, Miles came up to her, bearing a Lego piece in his hand. "Here, Momma," he said, "You missed this piece. Put it away with the others."

Now it was Alyssa's turn to cry.

The elders of the Orthodox Church have common phrase for what happened to Miles. They would say that he "came to a full *metanoia*." *Metanoia* is a Greek word meaning a change of heart, repentance, turning from one's sins, a change of way. It was one thing for Miles to realize what he had done wrong and to say, "I'm sorry." This is a big first step in the process of metanoia. However, it was quite a another thing for Miles to actively participate in his mother's discipline and make sure for himself that he did not hold on to even one piece of the Lego set she had temporarily taken from him. He was completely humble and showed a full, unreserved repentance.

There is a story of a Desert Father, Abbott Sisois, who at age one hundred was dying. For eighty years he had lived a life of repentance, but as he lay on his deathbed he asked the Lord for more time to repent. His disciples could not understand. "You are asking for time to repent, you who are the master of repentance?" He replied, "I'm only just beginning to learn the art."[44]

I struggle to appreciate this old saint's sentiments. Did he not believe after all those years that God had forgiven him? What kind of excuse for faith is that? Why does the Church uphold this kind of faith by repeating the story?

Since hearing how young Miles so thoroughly applied the art of repentance, however, I am beginning to see why Abbot Sisois felt he had not yet come to a complete change of heart. His was not a struggle to believe in God's forgiveness; rather, he understood that it takes time and constant work for crusty adults to return to having a child's soft heart.

Cunningness has not yet cluttered little children's hearts and minds. They are far more guileless than their elders. They have not yet built up layers of self-deception, self-justification, and denial. Their ego, even though focused squarely on themselves, is still highly sensitized to the possibility of focusing on God. As he grows older, it will be Miles' fate, as it is for everyone, to work continually to recapture his early openness.

Miles displayed the heart Jesus was so eager to see in his adult disciples. The would-be founders of the Holy Church greatly struggled to live out such humility, although they had the privilege of living with the humblest of men. They argued more than once about whom of them should be greatest in Christ's kingdom. Finally, Jesus picked out a little shaver like Miles and set him in front of these egocentric men. What he said next was blunt:

> I tell you the truth, unless you change and become like little children, you will never enter the kingdom of heaven. Therefore whoever humbles himself as this little child is the greatest in the kingdom of heaven.[45]

I suspect Jesus did not mean for me to take his message in a general sort of way—"Here now, lighten up and be more childlike." No, Jesus meant it for the nitty-gritty of everyday life. Block by block, I am to dismantle my tower of overweening pride so that I may instead realize with every component that *God* is my high tower and deliverer. I am to let go of each interlocking "Lego" of pride, envy, fear, rage, greed, covetousness, resentment, and judgmentalism. I must face the fact that as long as I live on this earth, I will always need to give up some aspect of sin. Eventually, I will experience full metanoia and enter body and soul into the Kingdom of heaven, because I will have made room for the Kingdom to come into me.

Here, Father God, I missed this piece. Put it away with the others.

# That Store Lady

*We may be grownups physically, but our souls are in many ways still adolescents. It is hard for us to believe that we are not the center of the universe.*

The Priest Michael

"We were here first!"

"Actually, I was here before you."

"No you weren't!"

"Yes, I was, but I'm not going to keep arguing because it's not worth it."

This exchange was not between a couple of adolescents. It happened at an Office Depot between two baby-boomers.

One day, I went there to buy supplies. I passed a middle-aged woman with what appeared to be her husband in the main aisle. "You don't want to buy that do you?" she snapped at him. Her features and voice were equally sharp. His shoulders and face looked ready to slide to the floor at any moment. He murmured, "I guess not."

I rolled my cart up to a store register behind a man in a wheelchair. I eventually realized the man was using the register to fill out an employment application, but not before the aforementioned couple had lined up behind me. As we moved to the next register, they got in line before me. The clerk was waiting on another person who had left some merchandise on the counter to obtain another item. The sharp faced lady asked the clerk, "You're not going to charge me for that stuff, too, are you? Because that's not mine!" He assured her he was not.

A new register opened, and the clerk invited us to move to his register. This time, I got in line first. The lady immediately cut ahead of me and said, "We were here first!" Well, she and I, the two baby-boomer-adolescents, had our little exchange of words.

My heart thudded and I felt the heat of fury course through me. The lady's selfish spirit was so front and center that it hit me like a punch in the nose. This person's whole posture while in Office Depot had been one of pure egocentrism. She assumed people were taking advantage of her to the extreme, and she was determined to protect her self-interests no matter how small the issue.

Once I got up to the cashier, he apologized for her behavior toward me. I tried to take the magnanimous view. "Well, if being first helped make her day, I guess she got what she needed." I did not completely mean it. I walked to my car and got in. "Lord," I prayed through clenched teeth, "Help me to forgive this selfish, mean-spirited, egocentric, childish, thoughtless woman."

Instantly, I realized that as different as she seemed from me, I who am "not nearly" as selfish and mean-spirited, the store lady was a mirror being held up to my face. She was so obvious with her self-centeredness that my own ego strongly reacted to it. My feelings of being violated and picked on reminded me how painful it is to others when I am being selfish, even if it is more subtle than this lady's blatant rudeness. Egocentrism has the effect of diminishing the place and value of others in order to promote and protect my self, as if that sort of false self is worth fighting for.

Diotrephes the cleric, "who loves to be first," reported St. John the Evangelist in his epistle, wreaked havoc and division on his church congregation.[46] My selfishness may seem less noticeable to me than either Diotrephes' or the store lady's, but it is at least obvious to God. It leaves in its wake a distinct, acrid unpleasantness. Moreover, my tightened gut and urge to swear when anyone cuts in front of me in the store, in traffic, or for accolades at work shows that God is not yet my full identity. In my heart, he is still too small.

It was disconcerting to discover that by middle age I still secretly think I am at the center of the universe. It certainly saddened my ego to learn once again that the world does not revolve around me. Painful or not, how good it was to cast off such rags of delusion. This realization, there in the Office Depot parking lot, became a sacrifice to God, an opportunity to lay down the burden of my false self. After all, left to my own ends, that store lady was just another version of me.

Lynette A. Smith

# Turn Over Every Stone

I am discovering that like many faith traditions, Christian and non-Christian, Orthodoxy encourages key spiritual disciplines, or *ascesis*, to cultivate personal growth. In the case of Christian development, the goal is to have the kind of fertile malleability that allows the Word of Christ (*Logos*) to dwell richly in me.[47] This Logos eventually develops me into a person of deep peace, truth, and loving magnanimity until my heart and mind dwell continually in God.

Disciplines such as prayer, fasting, almsgiving, worship, and patient waiting do not always appear to be effective tools for accomplishing such lofty goals. Sometimes I feel like I am digging through solid rock with a folding camp spade. Maybe the reason an ascetical practice seems so inadequate is because I am using it too sparingly—a modest picking here, a bit of scraping there, and I have not invested much faith in the process. When Jesus rebuked his disciples for having such inadequate faith, apparently it was smaller yet than a mustard seed, or he would not have brought up the issue. For with faith just the size of a mustard seed, he asserted, one can move a mountain of rocky ground.[48] Yet, is all the stir of rock and dirt worth it?

In my sophomore year, Mom and Dad bought a mobile home and rented a lot on one of the public school teachers' housing compounds in Shiprock, New Mexico. The lot boasted only packed gravel and sand, and no one would have looked down on Dad if he had never done anything with it. Many people did not plant lawns or gardens out in that sand; it took too much work and vigilance, and there was always the risk that nothing would survive. Any sizeable green areas in Shiprock had either been cultivated years ago or readily accessible to irrigation. Dad, however, wanted a patch of yard with a hedge around it to lessen the amount of grit sifting into our home during sand storms. He wanted to grow a few beans, squash, and tomatoes. I remember him pouring over Burpee's™ seed catalogue, studying which grass was the hardiest and which bush plantings he could coax into a low enclosure of protection. Within a shorter time than I thought possible, by force of faith, will, and hard work, Dad achieved his bit of blossom in the desert.

Metaphorically, I can welcome Christ as the tiller of my soul, infinitely more eager than my die-hard gardener dad to see my faith come to fruition. After all, it is not just me in the dirt, but Christ too, pulling up weeds, digging out stone, amending soil, heaven-bent on converting my desert into an oasis. Yet as pleasant as it is to contemplate the eventual outcome, the fact that Christ is such a relentless gardener causes a problem for me. The ground of my heart is so weedy, dry, and rock-ridden with sin; my progress is slow going and painful. I fear that with each pull of Christ's harrow I shall have to overturn every stone of pride, lift every longing to the light. To dig far enough below the surface, the tools—spiritual disciplines—that Christ wants to use must be far more substantial than my folding camp shovel. I do not relish this. I am not sure I possess enough faith to stand it. Much easier in the short run to scratch at the surface with a few coins in the charity donation box, scatter a few prayers around, and call it good.

I know it is no good, of course. Just as my dad needed to hope that his effort and persistence would pay off, I too, must believe that my cooperation—what the Orthodox Fathers call *synergy*—with Christ's work in me will bear fruit. If the ground of my stony heart is ever to be rich with the presence of the Logos, I must take the spiritual disciplines out of the shed and actually use them. Eventually, such faith might move a mountain's worth of rocks.

Lynette A. Smith

Voyage

# Marooned in the Stillest Place on the Planet

In 1999, John Haslett and three others decided to try out a sea route from Ecuador to Mexico that an ancient people, the *Manteño*, had used prior to the Spanish conquistadores.[49] Following the raft pattern of the Manteño, they built a two-story bamboo hut on top of nine sixty-one-foot-long balsa logs tied together and set off. Although they had obstacles to overcome, they felt one over-arching fear. The Gyre.

Haslett described this body of water as "a 600-mile-wide oceanic whirlpool," a ring-like system of ocean currents that revolves around a vortex in the Doldrums near Panama. The Pacific and Atlantic Intertropical Convergence Zone is a belt of calm and light baffling winds that sea merchants long ago came to dread, and called them doldrums because of the low spirits they found themselves in after days of no wind. When they catch a sailing vessel, it slows down, even threatens, the whole process of commerce. That is why favorable winds are called Tradewinds.

So if The Gyre caught Haslett's raft, it would not only prevent them from continuing the voyage, but they would be unlikely to survive without outside rescue. As Haslett put it, they tried hard to "sneak around this whirlpool" and "hug the coastline." It worked temporarily.

> Then The Gyre took over. We drifted in and out of it for a few days, always at the edge, always on the verge of entrapment, but with no wind to

51

move our ship, with no way to slip past it, we finally drifted in and began our relentless orbit.[50]

They endured nearly two weeks of an utterly calm ocean, deadly sea snakes, schools of hundreds of hungry sharks, rotting lines, and saltwater boils on their legs. While they were in the dinghy, their partially submerged raft nearly sailed away without them. In order to surmount each challenge, they divided the tasks by inclination and talent, calling themselves "Inventors," "Shark Police," and "Worker Bees." For each effort they put forth, they survived one more day, one more crisis. Haslett and his men hoped that when they arrived at the farthest north edge, they would catch a wind and break out. They never did. Finally, Haslett made a phone call to the Golfito naval base in Costa Rica, and the navy rescued them within fifteen hours.

In my life voyage, I have run into the doldrums many times. I know well how an acute case of depression can spiral into unremitting stagnation of mind, body, and spirit. The doldrums suspend the course of my best-laid hopes and plans. Floating through the days works for awhile. Get out of the lounge chair. Go to work. Walk around the lake. Write. Cook supper. Volunteer. Attend the Liturgy. Read the Bible. Pray. All that worthy effort keeps me alive long enough to know that there is one more thing I need to do.

I pick up the phone.

# NO SOLO VOYAGE

A few well-experienced people have attempted great solitary adventures: they set goals to fly, sail, or balloon around the world; climb Mt. Everest; and hike deep into the Amazon forest. Once the exploit begins, each of these brave souls appear to carry it out by themselves, but behind the scenes, a multitude helped to prepare them, right down to the makers of water bottles and trail mix.

In the spiritual journey—the greatest adventure of all—the truth is that I cannot, indeed, dare not travel the journey alone. Independent, individualistic American that I am, still I must take my life's voyage in the company of others. They obviously include my beloved husband, family, friends, and—less identifiable—all fellow Christians throughout the world. Moreover, I can rely on an unseen but deeply real dimension of fellowship and prayer with the saints who have gone on to paradise before me and dwell in Christ's presence. God sends other equally unseen but real beings—his angels—as messengers, guardians, and ministers of aid. Earth's creatures, too, can be my companions and teachers, or as Francis of Assisi would call them, my little brothers and sisters. The most essential companion of all is God himself, and learning to dwell with him in quiet and trust is the worthy odyssey of a lifetime.

Lynette A. Smith

# Those Invisible Lights

Thanks to revelations such as the late Alexandr Solzhenitsyn's *Gulag Archipelago*, Stalinist Russia is now infamous for its use of labor camps. Stalin created "special" camps where those deemed the most "incorrigible" of religious and political prisoners—both types labeled "politicals"—were lumped in together with the worst criminals. For the politicals, the threat of physical danger from the latter added tremendous threat to the already harsh conditions of the camp. These places were camps of death; to last even a few years was considered remarkable.

In 1939, the communists interned an art historian turned Orthodox priest-monk in such a special prison camp simply for being a good priest. Incredibly, this man, Father Arseny, survived for nineteen years at this camp until his release in 1958. A book of interviews and writings compiled by one of his spiritual children reveals what a remarkable man of God he was.[51] One time, he became ill and died, later reporting that his soul had left his body.

> While in this state...he saw the whole camp with all its prisoners and its prison guards as if from inside. Each person carried within himself a soul which was now distinctly visible to Father Arseny...Some were afire with faith which kindled the people around them;... others had only small sparks of faith and only needed the arrival of a shepherd to fan these sparks into a real flame. There were also people whose souls were dark and sad, without even the least a spark

of                                               Light.

> . . . Father Arseny was extremely moved. "O
> Lord! I lived among these people and did not
> even notice them. How much beauty they carry
> within them. So many are true ascetics in the
> faith. Although they are surrounded by such
> spiritual darkness and unbearable human
> suffering, they not only save themselves, but give
> their life and their love to the people around
> them, helping others by word and by deed."[52]

The identity of some of the people shining with light
astounded him. Here was a criminal, struggling to find a
better way to approach life than when the law had caught
up with him. There, unbelievably, was a prison guard, or
an administrator, who felt genuine compassion for the
captives and in order to help anyone, walked a razor edge
of risk to his own freedom.

Father Arseny wondered why he received this vision as he
was about to enter eternity. In answer, Mary, the Mother
of God, appeared to him and encouraged him that he was
not going to die, and that he could now return to the
camp knowing he was not alone. He would serve God
alongside these other lights. Just as his fellow prisoners
felt his flesh begin to get cold, Father Arseny's soul
reentered into his body; he coughed, shocking his would-
be mourners. Within two weeks he was back up and
around.

So far, neither God nor his angels have given me a view
of people's hearts such as Father Arseny received. I am
blessed enough if I receive insight into my own soul,
thank you. Yet once in a while—especially after reading

this man's story—I look at some one whom I have negatively judged to be a certain way and wonder. If I knew one particular narrative of her life, or heard one set of honest musings of her mind, would it change the way I thought about her?

Perhaps there is an invisible light inside even my most annoying, petulant coworker. He might be sending out clues now and again that this is so. Can I learn to be attentive enough to read them?

Perhaps with what candlepower God has graced me, I may help keep the smoldering wick of a discouraged friend from blowing out. That is, if I am willing to risk a little wind.

Perhaps, when people finally shut off the lights of the house, the computer monitors, TV screens, and iPods for a few hours of sleep every night, a nearly perceptible glow surrounds those who have cultivated some luminosity of the Holy Spirit, God's Uncreated Light.

During our Western Rite Matin prayers we recite the *Benedictus Dominus*, and the last stanza of this exquisite poem almost invariably strikes a tiny flame in me.

Through the tender mercy of our God
whereby the Dayspring from on high hath visited us,
to give light to those who sit in darkness
and the shadow of death,
and to guide our feet into the way of peace.[53]

Even when I am not completely aware that the Light is in me, or scarcely dare to believe it would come if I ask, the Spirit hovers, waiting for me over the gloaming.

Lynette A. Smith

# The Company of Angels

The closer that Father Arseny drew to God during his prison camp years, the more God gave him the gift of discernment. After the communists released him, former parishioners and others came to visit his home. Frequently, the visitor would no more step into his room, when the Father would ask a pointed question related to some issue known only to that person. Brought face to face with their suppressed inner fears, hopes, or sins, many of these people opened up to receive Father Arseny's counsel. They then went away with a greater ability to thrive spiritually in spite of an oppressive society.

The book's translator calls this level of discernment "clairvoyance," a common term found in other Orthodox stories of like-gifted saints. This term initially made me nervous, because it has come to mean a supernatural ability that a demonic power supplies an individual. For Orthodox writers in English, however, clairvoyance is simply what Webster's dictionary says it is: *the supernatural power of seeing objects or actions removed in space or time from natural viewing, and quick, intuitive knowledge of things and people; sagacity.* The context of tales of Christian clairvoyants indicates that the gift is from a holy God. If used with moral maturity and humility, it is a gift for the sake of others.

There is ancient precedent among the Hebrews for Father Arseny's gift. My favorite "clairvoyant" is the prophet, Elisha. Around the tenth century BC, he found himself in the position of keeping the current king of Israel out of political trouble with Syria.[54]

The king of Syria was at war with Israel. After conferring with his officers, he said, "I will set up my camp in such and such a place." The man of God [Elisha] sent word to the king of Israel: "Beware of passing that place, because the Syrians are going down there."

So the king of Israel checked on the place indicated by the man of God. Time and again Elisha warned the king, so that he was on his guard in such places. This enraged the king of Syria.

*Of course he would be angry!*

He summoned his officers and demanded of them, "Will you not tell me which of us is on the side of the king of Israel?"

*Who is the mole?*

"None of us, my lord the king," said one of his officers, "but Elisha, the prophet who is in Israel, tells the king of Israel the very words you speak in your bedroom."

*A huge security breach.*

"Go, find out where he is," the king ordered, "so I can send men, and capture him." The report came back: "He is in Dothan." Then he sent horses and chariots and a strong force there. They went by night and surrounded the city.

*Elisha is toast.*

When the servant of the man of God got up and went out early the next morning, an army with horses and chariots had surrounded the city. "Oh, my lord, what shall we do?" the servant asked.

"Don't be afraid," the prophet answered. "Those who are with us are more than those who are with them."

*Not since we last checked Dothan's census records.*

> And Elisha prayed, "O LORD, open his eyes so
> he may see." Then the LORD opened the
> servant's eyes, and he looked and saw the hills full
> of horses and chariots of fire all around Elisha.

Personally, I have never seen angels, or what the writer of
Hebrews calls "ministering spirits sent forth to minister
for those who will inherit salvation."[55] That does not
mean they are not close by ready to give assistance. Each
Sunday morning before the Processional to the altar our
priest prays,

> Graciously hear us, O Lord Holy, Father
> Almighty, Everlasting God: and vouchsafe to
> send thy holy Angel from heaven; to guard and
> cherish, to protect and visit, and to defend all who
> dwell in this thy holy habitation.[56]

Any idea that I am an isolated individual in the cosmos is
an utter illusion. I do not fight my battles by myself, and
even when loneliness lays its heavy ache in my chest, I am
not ever truly alone. No matter what evil the devils may
incite against the children of God, those who are with us
are more than those who are with the enemy of souls.

Lynette A. Smith

# Creatures at Communion,
# Or Balaam's Donkey

In the great and grand cathedral, near the high altar of our Lord, two humble mice have found where the unleavened bread of the Host is stored. Without pause for reflection, they bite down with sewing machine action. Before they can gorge themselves on the flaky food, however, a monk sends the cat to join the mice and distract them away from the feast. For now, at least.

Earlier, I wrote that the artistic beauty of the *Book of Kells* is a flowing yet bounded geometry of an intricate and ordered holiness. The book reveals another, and unexpected, creative expression. Tucked into textual and bordered spaces reside fairly uncomplicated drawings of creatures—

The hare,
> The horse
The stag,
> The lizard.
The otter,
> The rat.
The mouse,
> The cat.

And—heaven help me! Is that the Eucharistic Host the mouse is holding in its mouth and the calf has tattooed on its leg? How whimsical. How profane. Holy things are for the holy, after all.

However, contrary to my idea of propriety, quirky creaturely humor can be most holy, sprung as it is from the Creator himself. He, like the artists of the *Book of Kells*, inserts the odd joke into his communication with us, sometimes using animals to convey his punch line.

One of the most famous examples of this is the biblical story of the donkey that belonged to the prophet Balaam.[57] These two had a cordial life together until the donkey had to take him on a road trip to meet King Balak of Moab who wanted Balaam to put a curse on his enemy, the Israelites. God told Balaam to go, but not to curse the Israelites. Apparently, Balaam was feeling a little wishy-washy about what he would actually do for the Moabites. (They were dangling a nice paycheck in front of him.) So during the trip, the Lord sent an angel to reinforce his order that Balaam speak only what God would tell him.

It was not unusual for prophets to encounter angels from time to time; on this occasion, however, Balaam was clueless about his heavenly visitor. It was his donkey who saw the angel, and she did everything in her power to move out of the being's way. When the angel finally hemmed them into a narrow passageway, the donkey took the wisest course and lay down under Balaam. He, sensitive equestrian that he was, reacted to her unusual behavior by beating her.

At this ugly display, God opened the donkey's mouth to speak words, and she proceeded to let Balaam have it. Her logic was impeccable. "All these years that we've been together, have I ever done this to you before?" In other words, *I may be a donkey, but you are a jackass*. Balaam had to admit that he was the one who lacked awareness that something odd was causing the donkey's actions.

Only then did God open the prophet's eyes to see and hear the angel.

Maybe the difference in attentiveness between Balaam and his donkey is portrayed in the animal illustrations woven around the Gospel texts in the *Book of Kells*. Over the millennia, beasts have retained keen senses of smell, sight, or hearing, while we humans have lost the high levels of sensitivity we once possessed. Saint Paul described our situation this way:

> darkened in understanding,
> alienated from the life of God,
> because of ignorance
> due to blindness of hearts;
> losing all sensitivity,
> thus given over to mere sensuality,
> with an incessant lust for more.[58]

That is an immense loss to our quality of life.

If Paul's assessment is accurate, then my low level of receptivity to God's life could sure use a boost. Thankfully, God has provided for this need, above all—as the Western Rite Liturgy whimsically reads—in his "creatures" of bread and wine, changed by the Holy Spirit into the Body and Blood of Christ at the Eucharistic Supper.[59]

In the old medieval churches of Ireland, little mice understood of necessity that the closer they came to where the Communion Table stood, the more likely they would find the best source of nourishment around.

Do I?

Lynette A. Smith

# Séance-Free Communion
# With the Departed

Sunday, December 10, 2006 was the twenty-fifth anniversary of my dad's death. While doing the math the week before, for once I did not bear in mind how he died, or what a complex man and father he was. Orthodox tradition says the day of a Christian's death is the day of his or her birthday into heaven. I decided it was an occasion worth celebrating. After all, here is a man who started earthly life on December 6, wonderful St. Nicholas' Day, and began his heavenly life during Advent—the celebration of the coming of Christ into the world. How lucky can a person be?

Christians who celebrate Advent sometimes call it "Winter Lent," because they use the weeks before Christmas Day to reflect on the reasons God the Son deemed it necessary to become human. In the words of the *Te Deum*:

> When thou tookest upon thee to deliver man
> Thou didst humble thyself to be born of a Virgin.
> When thou had overcome the sharpness of death,
> Thou didst open the kingdom of heaven to all believers.

Once Jesus unlocked the entrance of the kingdom of heaven, all believers, whether they are dead or alive as far as this world is concerned, stay connected at an essential level. In fact, believers who are separated from others by death have the potential to become closer in spirit with the departed than when they were together on earth.

I admit that this is becoming true for my dad and me.

The Orthodox Church expects this to happen. She does not want me to I think I am utterly cut off from my father until the end of time. However, she makes clear that the union I have now comes not from attempting to "contact" him through séances or other esoteric means. Rather it is a result of Jesus' prayer in John 17 gradually becoming answered:

> [I pray] that they all may be one, as You, Father, are in Me, and I in You; that they also may be one in Us . . . Father, I desire that they also whom You gave Me may be with Me where I am.[60]

The Church explains the communion of saints this way:

> When Christians depart this life, they remain a vital part of the Church, the Body of Christ. They are alive in the Lord and "registered in heaven" (Hebrews 12:23). They worship God (Revelation 4:10) and inhabit His heavenly dwelling places (John 14:2). In the Eucharist we come "to the city of the living God" and join in communion with the saints in our worship of God (Hebrews 12:22). They are that great "cloud of witnesses" which surrounds us, and we seek to imitate them in running "the race that is set before us" (Hebrews 12:1).[61] Those in heaven with Christ . . . actively pray to God for all those in the Church— and perhaps, indeed, for the whole world. So we pray [request] to the saints who have departed this life, seeking their prayers, even as we ask Christian friends on earth to pray for us.[62]

So, after Liturgy that Sunday, I fed the congregation some of Dad's favorite earthly food. I brought Dad's college picture, and a placard that read:

> *He was a cookie monster, who also loved stew and cornbread.*
> *In memory of Roy Raphael Munger.*
> *May he rest in peace and may light perpetual shine upon him.*

There sure was a lot of smiling and lip-smacking going on in the parish! To tell the truth, sometimes I could not quite tell from where the pleasure was coming—parish, or paradise.

Lynette A. Smith

# Dr. Ephraim

It is the year AD 363. A wizened poet sits in a mountain cave overlooking the city of Edessa (now Urfa, Turkey). He has fled there because the Persians have invaded his home city, Nisibis, Syria, for the third time, and he needs a safe and solitary place to live, pray, and write. He spends a good deal of time in that cave, but often comes down to preach in Edessa. His sermons about God are so powerful that the congregation sometimes breaks down in sobs, and Ephraim has to stop speaking until they can hear him again.[63]

Famine strikes Edessa about ten years after Ephraim arrives there. He finds out that some people are hoarding food, and dismayed, confronts them. Lamely, they say they cannot find a way to dole out the food fairly. As old and shriveled up as he is, Ephraim jumps in and starts a food bank and a way to distribute the food.

In his hometown, he had been a schoolmaster and was such a prolific writer of poetry and hymns that folk nicknamed him "Harp of the Holy Spirit."[64] One account says,

> The originality, imagery, and skill of his hymns captured the hearts of the Christians so well, that Ephraim is given credit for awakening the Church to the importance of music and poetry in spreading and fortifying the faith.[65]

Ephraim wrote so abundantly and effectively on doctrine and other spiritual matters, that the Eastern Church translated many of his works from Syriac into Greek during his lifetime. Centuries later, the Western part of the Church gave him the rare title of Doctor. We in Western Orthodoxy commemorate him in June.[66]

Recently, I pulled out the bookmark I had made of one of Ephraim's famous prayers. It reads,

> O Lord, heal the wounds of my soul
> and enlighten the eyes of my mind
> that I may understand my place
> in Thine eternal design!
> And inasmuch as my heart and mind
> have been disfigured,
> may Thy grace repair them.

I like to think that this saint's designation as "doctor" is more than a title of theological scholarship. It also reveals a therapeutic role in encouraging me to return to our Original Nature.[67] Ephraim knows how much I need to be healed deeply of the wounds that the sins and the cares of this life inflict. Like Christ, he is concerned about the whole person, body, soul, and mind.

Dr. Ephraim, dwelling now in the heavenlies, pray for me.

# Silent Together with God

*Once the Curé d'Ars, a French saint of the eighteenth century, asked an old peasant what he was doing sitting for hours in the church, seemingly not even praying. The peasant replied: "I look at him, he looks at me and we are happy together."*[68]

Anthony Bloom

Christian religious services burgeon with words. In Protestant Evangelical churches, people expect extemporaneous prayers, abundant "praise and worship" songs, and meaty sermons (if they don't last too long). Although since Vatican II Roman Catholics have shortened their services (incidentally so have Episcopalians), still priests and parishioners must employ the quantity of words in the given liturgy, and the cleric must preach a sermon. In my tradition, the Western rite of the Orthodox Church, we celebrate a full Divine Liturgy rooted in ancient Anglican tradition, sing every verse to the hymns, and hear a homily. If anyone takes the cake on great slices of utterance, though, it would be our Eastern Orthodox brethren; for them a two to three hour Divine Liturgy is often par for the course and very little of it extemporaneous. We Christians have a lot to say and some of it is actually genuine worship. Except.

Our pastors tell us we need to go home, read the Bible and good "spiritual" books, and have a personal prayer time. My parents emphasized early on in my childhood that I should be so comfortable with the Lord that audible, impromptu prayer would be second nature. More words again, many of them good. Except.

Except when it is time to close the bibles, missals, and hymnals, and shut off the sound systems. Except when it is time to still our minds and tongues.

Although the Orthodox Church holds numerous weekly liturgical celebrations, especially during high holy days such as Lent, she holds this in healthy tension with a part of Tradition whose premise is quietness, or *hesychasm*, and encourages its personal use. *Hesychasm* is a mystical practice of experiential prayer, and its purists advocate dispensing with all outside sensory input while praying in this way. No bells or gongs, singers or songs, candles or incense, not even an icon; instead, practitioners turn the volume way down so they can contemplate God from the heart. Their words are few and pointed, "Lord Jesus Christ, Son of God, have mercy on me a sinner."

After Metropolitan Anthony told the story of the peasant in the cathedral I quoted above, he commented,

> That man had learned to speak to God without breaking the silence of intimacy by words. If we can do that we can use any form of worship. If we try to make worship itself out of the words we use, we will get desperately tired of those words, because unless they have the depth of silence, they are shallow and tiresome.[69]

I am learning to engage in hesychastic prayer a small piece at a time. I use to romanticize the contemplative, meditative life—what bliss must arise in these mystics' souls! I am a little more ambivalent now. On the one hand, to shut off the cacophony in my obsessive brain comes as a blessed relief. On the other hand, for one who has taken pride in loquaciousness and often tried to "make worship itself out of the words" I use, to persuade the cacophony to *stay off* is a frequent trial. Unfortunately, my brain focuses on getting the words correct only to lose consciousness of the One with whom I am supposed to be talking. To relinquish the right to formulate prayers in favor of simple quietness before God requires a stiff dose of self-denial. When I "speak to God without breaking the silence of intimacy by words"—that level of relationship asks something far different from me.

The silence of intimacy asks me to reach back to the preverbal child who has stilled herself on her mother's lap. The silence of relationship requires me to hole up with the grit-spitting prophet who listens in the cave for the nearly inaudible whisper. To invite silence into myself means that purveyors of words—theologian, philosopher, preacher, and teacher—must wait outside my heart's closed door. I turn within, determined to cut a trail through the tangle of words to a tryst with peace, the place of God's presence.

Lynette A. Smith

# LAND-LOCKED

At times, I just do not seem to make any progress. I am not so much voyaging as off-course in a land-locked wasteland. It is not unusual to encounter spiritual dryness, but in this case, the word wasteland is a misnomer, for in the desert experience my spirit may meet up with the crack-lipped Jesus out on his forty-day battle with temptation and self-denial. That would be no waste, but a consolation.

The Orthodox Church gives me a heritage in wisdom by way of ascetics who headed intentionally for deserts in Syria, Egypt, and Sinai beginning in the third century AD. They stripped themselves of all but the basic elements so that they could meet God at the core. Whether I live in a literal or spiritual desert (and I have done both), the Desert Abbas and Ammas (fathers and mothers) understood that the place takes on particular significance.

> Until one can get things outside himself, standing back from them, one cannot truly see them…Paradoxically, one cannot appreciate any reality, nor God's presence in it, until he can gain such distance. Then he can embrace it with a new attitude and perception of freedom.[70]

Desert experiences do not automatically work toward spiritual growth. "One must take care in the Desert or he will go mad," for the wilderness of the mind is a disturbing place where I fight demons and my own false selves.[71] Fallen humankind itself creates a merciless wasteland that strews its victims all over the globe. God calls me to work in synergy with him to do some part to bring renewal to this world, but eventually our parched condition will only give way when we see the returning glory of the Lord. Then, "The desert and the parched land will be glad; the wilderness will rejoice and blossom.[72]

## Peaceful Disturbance

The desert was silent. So profound was the silence, I felt its deep hum vibrate my subdural as if it was sending me sonar messages.

One spring, on our way to Phoenix, Arizona, my parents and I passed through the Sonoran Desert. The variety and abundance of plants, many in bloom, were too much to resist. Dad stopped along the road, and we began to wander through the unfenced land, marveling that a desert could be so lush. And throbbingly silent. I felt attracted and resistant at the same time; attracted to listen to the pulsating power that spoke without words; resistant to that energy, fearing its unrelieving presence would drive me mad. Did I really want that much silence?

Certain ascetics of Desert lore thought they did. Abba John tells about people who go off by themselves into the desert and become "so tantalized" by the unbroken silence of the desert that they are annoyed when brethren come to visit.[73] Abba John knows why. Instead of the desert providing them with spiritual growth, "they cannot stand the vastness of that silence which they themselves have courted," because "they do not even know the reason why solitude ought to be wanted and sought for." They have run off to the desert "without a well-matured purpose" chiefly to avoid dealing with other people.

The Abba must have been poking through my diary; I am still struggling to learn that solitude is not the same as isolation. Why then I should want solitude? As I wrote a few pages back, there is a beneficial silence in which I cease talking, turn my heart to God, and seek to enter into serenity. Solitude can settle me down to hear the small, nearly silent voice of the Holy Spirit and find inner strength.

Solitude can also make me crazy.

In our English language, we tend to equate silence with peace, but although a desert can be silent, it also holds an intensity that is not always peaceful, but disturbing. My short experience in the Sonoran taught me what the old ascetics before me learned: just because I may be able to achieve silence does not mean I will then live automatically in a state of serenity. There are at least two reasons why solitude can disturb me.

First, being truly alone with myself—no people, no distractions, no noise—may be unpleasant. What do I think about when I am not reading, watching TV, on the computer, listening to music, running to the store? Who am I outside the realm of my spouse, family, friends, church activities, and work? The answers to these questions may reveal a jumbled mind or a numbed sense of identity, or worse.

Second, going into solitude to seek God's presence within myself means war. First, I am going to do battle with myself and against evil. First, I am going to fight evil, because Satan hates me to allow in God. The precedence for contending with Satan comes from Jesus' wilderness visit "to be tempted by the devil," and later Christian ascetics followed Jesus' example to gain victory over demons as well as themselves.[74] The evil one will use every tactic possible to sidetrack me from my pursuit. I have known him to use my inclination toward the mystical to dazzle me with a mirage of "spirituality."

"Wouldn't it be a relief, Lynette, to simply shake off Church hierarchy and stuffy dogma and float free in your own specially made christian-buddhist-goddess-animist bubble?"

Mostly, though, Satan does not have to be so dramatic. Amma Theodora may as well be describing my usual struggle when she says, "You should realize that as soon as you intend to live in peace, at once evil comes and weighs down your soul through accidie (lethargy), faintheartedness, and evil thoughts."[75] She gives the example of an ascetic who, no sooner than he would try to pray, felt like he was coming down with the flu. However, the Amma promises, "If we are vigilant, all these temptations fall away."

Second, I am also going to do battle with myself to meet God at the core of my being. I have to engage the "who am I," "what am I thinking," questions, and fight through layers of false selves where I harbor broken attitudes, motives, and dreams. It is amazing how like Velcro my false selves are! Once I start peeling them away, I realize that there seems to be an endless supply of the spurious.

Sometimes I become fascinated with all my "issues"—the horror one enjoys. Under this scenario, the Desert Fathers teach it is best to dispense with solitude for a while and do some physical activity. Other times, I find the battle so discouraging I want to give up the whole project. Antiochian Metropolitan Philip counsels that I should persist, because:

> The 'Desert' is not only a valuable place; it is a condition of life...Without this condition of silence...our unsure feelings and emotions, our

twisted sentiments, remain tangled and confused...We remain a chaotic bundle...in which we never 'act,' but merely 'react'...[76]

Into my solitude, then, the Spirit of God wants to send his pulsating, silent energy—lovingly disturbing me—so that I will humbly rely on him for the kind of peace that guards my heart and mind. He wants to bring the kind of peace that returns me to sanity. A trip to a literal desert is not necessary to this struggle. However, it is an inevitable condition of being human that I face an "internal desert." I may as well acknowledge its value and let it inform my journey.

# A Consoling Wasteland

From ages ten through eighteen, I lived in Shiprock on the Navajo Indian Reservation in northwestern New Mexico. Besides working as educators in this desert town, my parents helped in the first Native American indigenous church of our denomination. Mom taught Sunday school to the young adults. She found out that cultural gaps between herself and them, and between the Bible and them, were stimulating challenges for her. It would be another decade before she traveled to the Holy Land, but while studying Bible atlases and illustrated encyclopedias, Mom realized one day that landscapes of the Bible and North America's Southwest are greatly similar. This insight provided her with a way of relating to an element of the traditional culture through comparing the life of a Navajo sheepherder of the Four Corners to a Hebrew Bedouin of the Sinai.

For my part, I instinctively wandered through my own type of Sinai, for what was true in that desert was also true in my world. The Southwest wilderness became what I wanted to avoid and yet so needed. It was a place of intense trial and silent solace. There, I saw my puny self meeting up with a creation easily able to snuff me out, but deigning to let me survive. One traveler to the Sinai could have been describing my life:

> Each step in the Sinai is at once a gift and a duty, a delight and a test, beauty and discouragement, joy and terror. The Book of Exodus has said all this… Together the Sinai and Exodus represent the universal parable of life, which is also a parable of faith.[77]

In the New Mexico desert, I cut my eyeteeth on a faith raw and gritty. It was a faith that let me lean my weight back, arms outstretched, into forty-mile-an-hour windstorms for whole seconds at a time. By the time I was eleven, on Sunday afternoons the desert would draw me outside into itself. I would zip up a hoodie to protect my sensitive ears, clutch a walking stick stripped of bark, and head across the tumbleweed field south of the teachers' housing. For moments, I could stride up the sandy path at an even pace. Then a wind gust would shove my shoulder, pushing me sideways. I would right myself only to take such a blast of sand to the face, it left a grainy imprint on my lips. Like a landlubber aboard ship, I lurched my way through the wind's gauntlet, head down, bell-bottoms whipped up into flags.

My route was nearly always the same. I ducked through the hole in the barbed wire fence at the end of the school district property, turned east onto a sand-rutted road that ran wherever a pickup truck wanted it to go, then left it to meander south again. There, my feet crunched on more solid ground, a conglomerate of pebbles, bits of shell and coral. I was treading on the carcass of a thirty million year old ocean. In death, this spot of the San Juan Basin had surrendered its remains to the Shiprock gravel pit.

As I walked down into the pit—vacant on Sundays— mounds of texture rose to my left and right: mini-Saharan dunes; pebbled breasts; and cement culvert graveyards. When tired from roaming between them, I would find the sheltered side of a sand heap and lay back against its slight yield. There I contemplated the vault slung wide and far overhead where clouds seldom interrupted the ubiquitous purple. Eventually I would sit up and drop my gaze to the sky's edge.

When I first took my walks, to my naïve eye the desert's barrenness reached horizon to horizon. Even cactus, sagebrush, and yucca had scorned this place as too arid for survival. In time, insatiable hope for signs of life taught me to find them.

In spring, rains resurrected dormant seeds of wild geranium, marigold, and jimsonweed. Three weeks and no showers later, I mourned the crackle of their death under my heels. If I sat stone still, tiny lizards dashed over my shoes or meditated in my shadow. Once, the flash of a fox sent my usually sedentary legs pumping up and down jagged hills just to prolong the sight. On summer evenings, walks might be punctuated with ground owls standing at their holes—small, fluffy exclamation points on cracked parchment.

Invariably after my visit to the gravel pit, my feet led me further south and slightly east to the mesa's edge. Directly below me ran a wide cement irrigation canal that brought water to thirsty fields of alfalfa, corn, and squash. Not far from the canal, children and lambs played outside a hogan. As I watched, a father or uncle might drive up to the little compound in their truck; I wondered if they ever looked up and saw me. Probably.

From here, I looked down on a slightly more lush land hugging the tree-lined San Juan River that wound its ribbon through the main part of town. Almost directly before me I saw the green rectangle of the high school's football field, the Catholic Church, the Foutz Trading Post. Turning to the west, I followed Highway 64 as it bridged the river, climbed up its bank, and curved south again. On that side of town, teenage boys were likely making eyes at the cute girls in KFC, or if they were "stomps," plying their cowboy techniques on a bronc at the Navajo Rodeo grounds. Tan and brown stuccoed houses built by the Navajo Housing Authority huddled on the upper south plains, and in the haze beyond them lay the long stretch of Table Mesa.

What held my gaze, though, was the monolith standing sentinel twelve miles to the west, the Ship Rock itself, patron of the town. In the nineteen century, white explorers beheld the ancient volcano throat jutting sixteen hundred feet above the desert floor, and saw in its massive base and eroded angles, the shape of a clipper in full sail. The Navajo call it *Tsé Bit'a'í*, Winged Rock.

The tuft cone has two ragged walls of petrified remains running perpendicular to it that certainly reminds one of a giant bird who, wings outstretched, had plunged itself into the earth. Legends of the rock's origin and significance vary, but all reveal a sense of awe it commands. Whether one agrees with many Navajo that Tsé Bit'a'í is sacred, the Rock undeniably broods with mystery. Several times, I had driven with family members up to the base and craned my neck to let its sheer glory overwhelm me, until dizzy with the sensation that the Rock was sailing me through the sky.

I preferred to view the Rock from my perch by the gravel pit, for there I could catch its moods. Sunsets particularly accentuated its grandeur. On clear evenings, as it slipped behind the distant Lukachukai mountains, the sun etched the Rock and nearer badlands in brilliance and shadow. One sunset, rare clouds bounded the Rock in rolling waves of crimson and gold, seeming to bear it, and me, toward infinity.

Out in the desert, I was who I was. No one was there to tease me for being a "honkey" or for my oddities, my unathletic and skinny body. Simply a part of the landscape, I confessed into the wind my paucity, fears, and dreams. The wind, as faithful in its power to carry as to buffet the soul, threw my cry up to God.

God.

I did not become a pantheist. Even so, God seemed to mother me in the sky's womb. Somehow he really was my Rock, a cleft hiding me in its wings. By sixteen, I was questioning my acceptability in the world, and mental agony would tempt me to end my life soon enough. Yet day after day the desert never refused my presence, the sky never shut me out, the Rock always let me gaze into its shadows. They were divine graces delivering a silent promise, steadfast amid the encroaching howl.

When I graduated from high school and left literally for greener pastures, no matter. The desert never left me.

Lynette A. Smith

# Mt. Desolation

Elijah the prophet was so spiritually endowed, he is one of the few biblical people who go on record as being "translated" straight to the heavens instead of dying the old fashioned way.[78] When Jesus is transfigured on Mt. Tabor eight hundred years later, Moses and Elijah appear and talk with him, representing the Law and the Prophets who predicted the Messiah.[79] The New Testament and the Church honors Elijah as the foretold prototype of John the Baptist who would prepare people's hearts to receive the Messiah's coming.[80]

Elijah has not always been so dynamic a personality, however. After he completes a successful, fiery, pro-Yahweh campaign on Mt. Carmel, he finds himself fleeing for his life from the furious Baal worshipper, Queen Jezebel, to the wilderness of Mt. Sinai, otherwise known as Mt. Horeb, or "Desolation," nearly a thousand miles away.[81] Some two hundred miles into his escape, he slumps down under a bush and prays to die. Exhausted not only from running but also depressed from the huge letdown from victory to grave danger, he falls asleep. An angel feeds him then sends him on the rest of his journey. Whether or not the prophet had intended initially to go so far away into the utterly desolate, jagged mountainous area of Horeb, nevertheless, he winds up there. He spends a night in a cave and sometime in the early hours of the morning, Yahweh sends his word into his heart. God asks a curious question for an omniscient Being, but it is one designed to give an extremely stressed man a chance to get things off his chest. "What are you doing here, Elijah?" Elijah readily pours out his heart.

My own story barely raises the pulse next to Elijah's tale of fire from heaven, hair-raising intrigue, and threatened assassination. Yet both he and I know what it is like to stand on heights of potential achievement only to be plunged into depths of desolation. My penchant for public speaking, a good singing voice, cross-cultural experience, and an education in biblical studies certainly lent credibility to an overseas missions call. When I sang during visits to Pentecostal churches, the congregation would on occasion weep and raise their hands and voices in praise to God, producing an emotional high from which I was loathe to come down. I took these times as small affirmations that I was on the right track. God was using *me*.

When I hit bottom in that little Bangkok apartment, my songs splintered into a hundred cries for death. After all the prayers, counseling, strenuous mission selection process, and colossal struggle to raise funding, I had "arrived," but then could not cope. This was supposed to be my Mt. Carmel. Though I figured it was an over statement at the time, I would have liked the prediction of the pastor at one of my supporting churches to come true. "When the soles of your little feet stand on the tarmac of Bangkok's airport, the power of the Holy Spirit will fill you and you will do mighty things for God." None of that happened; instead, I fell apart. Instead, the Thai leader of my denomination saw me at the mission's headquarters one day, looked me in the eye, and said, "What are you doing here?" What, indeed. I fled from Bangkok to hole up in a small Denver apartment, away from the press of "the ministry," and tried to repair.

Back in Elijah's cave, he hears God tell him, "Go out and stand on the mountain…for my Presence is about to pass by." God sends a spectacular display of wind and fire most people would take to be his presence. Elijah, though, is not impressed; he is tired of external demonstrations of power. He wants deep inner assurance that God has not abandoned him. Not until Yahweh talks to him in a small intimate whisper does he come out of his cave, and the ensuing conversation with God rebuilds Elijah's confidence in himself and in the Lord's guidance.

I took much longer than Elijah did to take God's reassurance and straighten out my life. Sometimes I wonder, "Did I have to drip sweat and tears under a Thai sun order to begin redefining my sense of purpose?" Well, did Elijah have to run all the way to Sinai in order to renew his? Only God knows. What I do know is that God used our wind-blasted despair to hollow out in each of our hearts a cave where, depleted and mute, we could hear his murmur of hope.

Lynette A. Smith

# Constant Companion

"You're going to have to accept the fact that you have the back of an old lady," my doctor (a general practitioner who shall remain nameless) told me. I received this heartening opinion after he had read my MRI results that revealed a forty-two year old back riddled with arthritis and several shrunken discs. Originally I had requested the scan because my neck bothered me so much I worried that another cervical disc was about to explode.

By twenty, I had incurred a series of freak accidents scattered throughout childhood and youth, including flying over the handlebars of a ten-speed. After enduring five years of increasing neck pain and decreasing mobility, Lynn Wilson, a neurosurgeon in Farmington, New Mexico, put me under his high-powered microscope and picked out the pieces of one of my cervical discs. Once he had opened up my neck, all he had to do was touch the disc with his instrument, and as he told me later, "It fell apart like jelly."

Wilson had been initially reluctant to perform the surgery, but once he conducted a myogram, a test for muscle and nerve weakness, it became clear that nerves in my neck were severely damaged. Now I had his attention; if he did not perform a fusion of the vertebrae, even a minor accident, such as whiplash, would likely turn me into a paraplegic. With all the risks of the procedure set before me, I gulped, said yes, and have been thankful for it ever since. I have fewer episodes of acute pain in my neck today than when I first stepped into Dr. Wilson's waiting room, and I escaped paralysis. One caveat, though. In about twenty years, he said the cervical disc below the fusion might suffer from bearing the loss of motion above. Thankfully, the MRI taken those twenty years later did not reveal any problem with the next disc. It just confirmed what I already knew—barring a miracle, the pain I had borne for more than half my life was going to remain a constant companion until the day I died.

As anyone who suffers from chronic pain will testify, it invades everyday life. It wakes me up in the night, yells for attention when I am driving, throws tantrums in the grocery store, and cries during church. Too soon, it grows impervious to medication. Although mountain vacations, humor, lovemaking, or tearjerker movies are good analgesics, I cannot distract chronic pain for long. It restricts employment choices and interrupts periods of creativity. In short, chronic pain is rude.

In the sixth century, St. Gregory the Great expressed his frustration with illness. It has a familiar ring:

> It is now almost full two years that I have been confined to my bed, afflicted with such pains of gout that I have hardly been able to rise on feast-days for as much as three hours space to solemnize mass. And I am soon compelled by severe pain to lie down, that I may be able to bear my torment with intervening groans. This pain of mine is sometimes moderate, and sometimes excessive: but neither so moderate as to depart, nor so excessive as to kill me.

Constant pain also toys with the mind. Never having been athletically inclined, it becomes one more reason not to make a physical effort to increase strength and mobility.

"Better not move," it yelps when I think about going for a walk. "Remember how your thoracic feels like someone is shooting darts at it when you walk." So I do not budge from the computer…and wind up feeling like a dartboard anyway.

Where has God been in the business of my physical affliction? Sometimes I have sensed his reassuring nearness, such as when I waited in the hospital room for surgery. In the first three months of recovery, I wound up reading the Bible through. At times during the reading, I felt in my body, even to the top of my head, as though I were lifted above all pain and suffering. God was in his heaven and yet here in the world. He would eventually make all things right.

Balmy seasons thereafter have been less frequent. Rather, prosaic seasons trudge on day after day, in which I have no emotional sensation that God is anywhere but far away in his heaven. I commiserate with others—which brings comfort—but the dry winds of daily pain create a deserted place no one else can really share. Then the Psalms, the pain medication for the soul beloved for centuries by Jew and Christian alike, become a mainstay. A Semitic idiom for "strength" is "bones," and so I particularly appreciate poets who implore God to attend to the precarious state of their bones:

> Do not hide Your face from me
> in the day of my trouble…
> For my days are consumed like smoke,
> And my bones are burned like a hearth…
> I am like a pelican of the wilderness;
> I am like an owl of the desert.[82]

Reportedly, chronic pain can be converted into a wise teacher of endurance, patience, and even creativeness. I presume endurance plays a part in my high threshold for pain in general, and sometimes I tough out difficult situations long after it might have made ordinary sense to do so.

Patience comes and goes; occasionally my husband is privileged to hear me complain how tired I am of my inadequacies and how guilty I feel that my physical upkeep makes a dent in the family wallet. In fact, why do I have to endure this malady in the first place? Frankly, I am land-locked by limitations that force me to either persistently innovate or whither in anger and self-pity. So, with loved ones' encouragement, I try to develop an ascesis that shows proper respect for my back, and resolutely test various methods until I find the current combination of therapy and exercise that persuades the pain to simmer down.

In regard to creativeness, I suppose this book is an offering to that. As Bedouins of the Sinai or sheepherders of the American Southwest have learned to create refuge and see beauty in a harsh environment, I can and must make a home in the wilderness of my body.

I believe the Holy Spirit also gives a particular kind of strength that sustains me to explore innovation and regular attitude adjustment. It is a sixth sense, a soul sense beyond reason or emotion that Christ is not only always present, but actually abides in my suffering with me, and bears it in his own body. Admittedly, some days it sounds trite to believe this, but deep down I know it is true: pain may be my constant companion on the journey, but so, too, is the Lord.

# Laugh, O Barren Woman

During the Holy Saturday service in which I became a member of the Orthodox Church, my priest called me by a new name, Sarah. The practice of choosing the name of a biblical or Christian saint is an ancient tradition affirming connection with the Church as one's spiritual family. Parents select children's names for them, but an adult like me will choose for herself a saint with whom she has an affinity. I chose the Old Testament matriarch, Abraham's wife. My priest encouraged me to "get to know Sarah," and I knew he did not mean merely to read her story in the scriptures, but to develop a deep spiritual bond with her. I gave a start of pleasant surprise; I had secretly been doing just that for years, and here he was validating it out loud.

Sometime in my budding adulthood, Sarah's story struck me, although she and I could not be more different. Probably the only commonality is that a family member higher up on the chain of authority told us one day that we were moving to a new, drier part of the country and better pack our bags. I live far from Sarah by eons, events, location, language, ethnicity, and culture. Yet, something about her leaps over the chasms to connect with me here and now.

In the Genesis narratives, Sarah is the first woman after Eve who has some of her words recorded. The first instance is implied rather than quoted; she boldly lies to the Pharaoh for her husband's safety, saying that she is only Abraham's sister, and barely gets out of the palace before the monarch beds her. Apparently, she was

97

irresistibly gorgeous. The next scenarios involve telling Abraham to impregnate Hagar as a surrogate mother, since she could not have children herself. Although a son is born as Sarah planned, the relationship sours between the surrogate and her, and Sarah tyrannizes Hagar until she and the child run off into the desert. God will have none of that, so Sarah finds she must put up with Hagar and son a little while longer until she has another opportunity kick them out for good.

Abraham was always moving Sarah from one desert's edge to another, camping at oases and wells. Once when he could have taken the "well-watered plain of Jordan," he allowed his nephew to have it while he and Sarah went on to lesser green pastures. Sarah never seems bothered to live in these places.

Her barrenness was of another kind.

The most positive, touching words from her involve the turning of this barrenness. When one of three visitors announces she will get pregnant at age ninety, Sarah laughs incredulously to herself, "After I have grown old, shall I have pleasure, my husband being old also?" The messenger and she have an amusing exchange—he teases her that she laughed, she denies it, and he chides her, "Is anything too hard for the Lord?" Once her son is born, Sarah exalts, "God has made me laugh, and all who hear will laugh with me," so naturally they name the boy, Isaac, "Laughter."

The Church and its scriptures view Sarah as a holy woman. After all, she is the biological ancestress of Jesus. The Apostle Peter tells Christian wives they are Sarah's daughters if they cultivate the inner beauty of a gentle, quiet spirit, do good, and do not let themselves be intimidated.[83] A beloved icon of Orthodoxy called, "The Hospitality of Abraham," shows both he and Sarah presenting food to the three visitors, understood to be an epiphany of the Trinity. Thus, to the Church, Sarah is standing within great holiness, yet Genesis does not record she ever leaves her tent. Is the Church's portrayal the same Sarah I know from the Old Testament? Peter has one thing right; she does not let anyone bully her. Otherwise, Old Testament Sarah appears to have had limited faith, is more outwardly than inwardly beautiful, and is neither gentle nor calm. By presenting both accounts, however, the Church implies that I am right to be drawn to Sarah.

Why exactly does she mean so much to me? Perhaps I intuited in my twenties that I would not bear children. Am I attracted to Sarah because she was once barren, or that she finally bears? Certainly her barrenness does not diminish her in my eyes, but settles her deeper in my heart. The fact that she does go on to bare Isaac even after her ovaries have shriveled to raisins demonstrates to me that fecundity is directly from God's heart, whether he brings it to a woman's body, a desert, or to empty places in my soul.

Do I enjoy her self-willed and manipulative personality? Not so much. One New Testament writer notices the flip side of her character flaws, however. Possibly interpreting her snickers inside the tent as a small wellspring of hope, the writer says she "judged God faithful who had promised."[84] Sarah uses her calculating bent to deduce from the conversation with the visitor that Abraham's God really meant to include her personally in his blessing.

I like the Church's assessment of a clearly flawed saint. She is a Saint with imperfections, as am I, and her life teaches me to embrace the authenticity of my humanness. Occasionally when I feel dried up and unfruitful in my work, I say, "St. Sarah, pray for me!" and I can almost see the set of her jaw as she sizes up the situation and asks God to give me the gift of "laughter." I believe God hears her, for when he appraises Sarah's life in its whole, he sees what I pray he will also see in me: "blessings shaken out of an imperfect life like fruit from a blighted tree."[85]

# Whiffs of Mercy

Dry, choking drought in Shiprock again. Just inside the northeastern edge of Navajo country, the town is in the geological bowl of the dried up San Juan Basin. Except for the thin, green threads of irrigation and the San Juan River running through it, it is a shallow basin perpetually empty of rain. Evergreens are hard put to grow in Shiprock even with substantial hand watering. One has to drive out some way toward the high mesas to find where soil and weather give juniper and piñon a natural chance to thrive.

How much then, when outside playing of an evening as a child, a rare whiff of rain on evergreens tantalized my senses. The scent came from far away, floating out of a storm passing the town by, whose clouds I might not even see. Eventually, a few times in the year, a mercy load of down slope winds from the Chuska range in the west or Sleeping Ute Mountain to the north brought more than mere hints of distant moisture. A sudden tantrum of rain would hurl itself into Shiprock's bowl, providing, for all the fury, a fraction of an inch of moisture. A spatter of promise fulfilled; better than nothing, less than sufficient.

This reminds me of how small humanity's redemptive efforts seem in the face of the world's vast wasteland of needs. If we deliver the persecuted of Dafor, we must also relieve the oppressed in Afghanistan, and shelter the mentally ill indigents roaming the streets of Denver. If we build housing for Hurricane Katrina or Haitian earthquake victims, we must not then neglect our sisters who suffered rape last month. For every discovery of a cure for a disease, we must struggle to ameliorate dozens more. When I consider the immense challenges the world presents, I grow almost numb with discouragement.

I am like the little boy who put his finger in the hole in the dike, only to discover the sea has found another crack, and another. My finger is better than nothing, but it is far less than sufficient. The world needs, as an old song goes, "Somebody bigger than you and I." Such reflection invariably provokes the well-worn questions, "If there is a God of love, why doesn't he do more to take care of his creation?" "Where is the promise of his coming?"[86]

The dilemma is one reason I find Old Testament scripture attractive. God risks his good reputation, and he allows people to go public in their frustration with his apparent passivity and neglect during horrific situations. He does not sweep the reality of human-divine tension under some theological rug. One biblical poet, Asaph, is especially good at giving voice to this frustration. After the Babylonians destroys Jerusalem and the Temple in 586 BC, this survivor does not hold back.[87]

> Why have you rejected us forever, O God?
> . . . Turn your steps toward these everlasting ruins,
> all this destruction the enemy has brought
> on the sanctuary.
> . . . We are given no miraculous signs,
> no prophets are left,
> and no one knows how long this will be.

Then to remind himself—and God—how God is truly in charge of all creation, Asaph sings,

> But you, O God, are my king from of old;
> you bring about salvation upon the earth.

. . . It was you who set all the boundaries of the earth;
you made both summer and winter.

However, like a little spattering of rain on parched earth, remembering the past is not quite enough to satisfy Asaph's heart. His intercessory desert chant rises and rises in passionate plea:

Do not hand over the life of your dove to the wild beasts;
do not forget the lives of your afflicted people forever.
Have regard for your covenant,
because haunts of violence fill the dark places of the land.
*Rise up, O God, and defend your cause.*

No less than Jerusalem's ruined temple, the sanctuaries of this earth—and of our souls—crack and crumble from a dearth of wisdom, justice, love, and humility. I am reassured, then, to hear of a rumor circulated in Orthodoxy that down through the ages, God has hidden monks of prayer in the secret of the hills, who, like Asaph of old, continually intercede for this world. They pray, "Lord Jesus Christ, Son of God, have mercy on us sinners," until the time when Jesus Christ will return to depose the evil one and to renew the earth completely.[88]

Occasionally, usually when I least expect it, my nostrils almost catch the incense of those prayers—whiffs of God's mercy—drifting over my head.

Lynette A. Smith

# DYING TO LIVE

If the Kingdom of Heaven transcends earthly dimensions, surely the Christian idea of death also embodies mystery. Maybe death is even one of the greatest paradoxes of all. The writers of Scripture and the Holy Fathers have no trouble taking on death's paradox and ambivalence, and I would doubt their honesty and helpfulness if they avoided the subject. Unlike them, though, I am tempted to leave this uncomfortable and difficult issue out of my quest for God. Yet to ignore it actually removes the possibility of fulfilling that quest.

With one voice the Church's wise ones teach that death necessarily comprises two modes. The first form, "bodily death," everyone recognizes, and comes at the end of earthly life. The second type, "living death," is more obscure, and to be enacted every day of the trek in this world. Successful passage into the Kingdom of God necessarily involves my bodily death and my living death.

While my mind and will stumbles over this reality, my heart often vibrates to the sacred chant of one godly saint after another who affirms this to be true. These saints, whether from the Bible, early Church times, or today, are not morbidly fixated on death. Rather, they take Jesus' words and example seriously: one dies in order to live. I will only fully live out the journey as I die to myself and surrender to Christ's venture, now and in the life to come.

Lynette A. Smith

# Which Metaphor is Mine?

Without metaphors, I do not communicate well for long. Metaphorical language provides a frame for interpreting my life and world, and I especially rely on it when I need to conceptualize the invisible God and relationship with him. Jesus, his Apostles, and the Church's fathers understand this reality and draw on a wealth of imagery to describe the abstract process of dying to oneself to become fully alive in Christ.

Jesus invites people to take his yoke on their shoulders and learn from him.[89] He claims his true servants will be just like their master: grains of wheat that do not bear fruit unless they fall into the ground and die.[90] Along other agricultural lines, he stresses to his disciples, "I am the vine, you are the branches. He who abides in me, and I in him, bears much fruit; for without me you can do nothing."[91] Jesus' most often quoted metaphors are: deny yourself, pick up your cross, and follow me; the one who wants to gain his life had better learn how to lose it first.[92]

St. James exhorts, disrobe yourselves of moral filth and evil so that you can accept the *Logos* deep within the soul.[93] The Apostle Peter likens the testing of believers' faith to the refining method a chunk of gold ore endures.[94] St. John echoes a line from Jesus' words to his disciples prior to his death that we can know that we have passed from death to life when we truly love the brethren and are willing to lay down our lives for them.[95]

The Apostle Paul creates an exhaustive list of metaphors, all of them graphic. He lifts Jesus' metaphor of cross-bearing several feet in the air: believers not only take up their cross, but are taken up onto the cross, crucified with Christ and no longer live to themselves.[96] He instructs his congregations to "put to death" any part of their nature that involves sin.[97] He visits a clothier and compares the sinful and Christ-like natures to an old man in worn out clothing needing to strip buck-naked and put on a whole new outfit, to become a new man.[98] Spiritual ascesis works similarly to a prizefighter's self-discipline: "I do not box as one beating the air; but I harden my body and subdue it..."[99] Each Christian is a runner competing against his or her own past loss and achievement to win the trophy of "the upward call of God in Christ Jesus."[100] All believers participate in a marathon running team with Christ as the pacesetter. To run as aerodynamically as possible, they "throw off everything that hinders and sin that so easily entangles."[101] They follow the example of Jesus, the leader and finisher of their faith, "who for the joy that was set before Him endured the cross, despising the shame, and has sat down at the right hand of the throne of God."[102]

Several early Church Fathers use Old Testament Jacob's vision of a ladder to illustrate the spiritual life. St. Gregory of Nazianzus, eulogizes his friend St. Basil for ascending Jacob's ladder "by successive steps towards excellence."[103] In his homily on John 15, St. John Chrysostom suggests, "The ladder seems to me to signify in a riddle…the gradual ascent by means of virtue, by which it is possible for us to ascend from earth to heaven, not using material steps, but improvement and correction of manners."[104] St. Jerome writes, "The Christian life is the true Jacob's ladder on which the angels ascend and descend, while the Lord stands above it holding out His hand to those who slip and sustaining by the vision of Himself the weary steps of those who ascend."[105] St. John Climacus develops the metaphor to the greatest heights. His nickname, "Climacus," or ladder, bears the signature metaphor of his book, *The Ladder of Divine Ascent*, and he divides the book into thirty steps, or rungs, one climbs to come into perfect relationship with the Holy Trinity.

I revel in these metaphors, but I am also overwhelmed with their sheer range. In pondering these many symbols over the years, I have wondered, "Which metaphor is mine?" Which image should I adopt for my theosis? Am I a grain of wheat, a hunk of gold, an athlete, or a ladder climber? Should I get aggressive with myself and kill off sinful behaviors, or do I "merely" remove them and replace them with virtues? Do I pull my cross behind me, or hang upon it? It is not helpful to answer, "all of the above," for then the many options paralyze my motivation. Sometimes I have wished the Holy Scriptures and Tradition of the Church would have stuck to one image, in compassion for those of us with obsessive-compulsive disorder.

However, as I ponder this dilemma, I am coming to believe the answer actually resides in the very multiplicity. Since God desires me to return from where I have fallen to my place in his eternal design, I need all the assistance possible to engage the process of return. These metaphors speak to my identity; they help me situate myself in relationship to Christ. British musicologist, Liz Garnett, writes about the value of metaphor in songs, "When people recognise metaphors that resonate with their own experience in a direct and immediate way, they make the music their own."[106] Possibly, then, the Church provides manifold metaphors to accommodate people's varied situations and experiences. She wants to encourage them to visualize how they may make Christ's life their own. My farming grandmother (God rest her soul) probably gleaned the most when she read the agricultural similes; whereas, construction workers may perk up when they hear about St. John's *Ladder*.

For me, it all depends. Days dawn in which I stumble to the kitchen for a cup of coffee, wanting nothing better than to doze back off to sleep. Athletic metaphors— turned literal—serve me well then; I exercise to awaken the body and mind so that I can turn my will toward prayer. When critical or angry, it helps to visualize leaning back on the cross, arms outstretched, relinquishing the right to judge. Anxiety and distress constantly muffle joyous creativity and stifle impulses to renew my love for God; thus, the disrobing motif vividly illustrates that I must remove strip by strip these stinking rags, as Martha unbound her resurrected brother from his burial clothes.

Which metaphor is mine? Whichever one best sends its message, at the moment of challenge, to die a little more to myself and live in Christ.

# Therapeutic Tree

*Unless a grain of wheat falls into the ground and dies, it remains alone. But if it dies, it produces much grain. He who loves his life will lose it, and he who hates his life in this world will keep it for eternal life.*[107]

Jesus the Christ

As a young woman, this parable of Jesus impressed me greatly, and I identified myself as the grain of wheat that must die. Two drawings evolved out of my efforts to express this. The first was an abstract portraying a large plant growing from a seed. The seed is under high distress: four long, crisscrossed thorns stab through its sides and a gashed front exposes a tiny cross. Out of the seed blood drips into the reddened ground from which a root system spreads. The seed and its plant hang in white space. A cold, harsh rendering; its one redeeming feature is that the bud and roots outsize the other aspects. It frightened me, so I drew a second, less abstract picture, locating the seed logically underground and without thorns. The seed is twice larger than the first and a wooden cross thrusts its four ends through it as if bursting from a grave. Again, blood drips from the bottom of the cross-seed to form a root system. Out of the top of the cross above ground grows a single plant with a small bud ready to unfold in rays of light streaming from a blue sky. The colors are more natural, edges rounded, and objects two-dimensional. This time seed, cross, and roots are much larger than the plant. Overall, a warmer, more hopeful, and inviting picture than the first, I thought.

In retrospect, I suspect a combination of painful personal events, physical illness, and religious training influenced my interpretations. In the first picture, only by my excruciating suffering can I produce burgeoning fruit, while the cross of Christ plays a diminished role. In picture two, the cross diminishes the role of my suffering but produces only conservative fruit. Though the second depiction conveys a more balanced illustration of Jesus' parable than the first, both pictures fail to recognize the life-bringing power of his death.

In the ensuing years, I continued to agonize over how to be the seed that dies to produce "much grain" and properly "hate my life in this world in order to keep it for eternal life." How much I wanted to love Christ and trust the Holy Spirit to make me pure through his indwelling presence. This issue of personal purity stalked my thoughts, words, and actions. Many days were fraught with anxiety to be perfect as God is perfect so that I can be a good witness to the "unsaved" by word and deed. When I fell down on the job, which of course was a frequent reoccurrence, I berated myself unmercifully. My faith tradition rightly taught that I should ask Jesus for forgiveness and in his grace he would grant it, which I did frequently and privately. Yet the "joy of sins forgiven" did not ease my soul for long.

For a while, I fantasized that the physical, mental, and social pain I endured would end in glorious martyrdom. Barring that, hopefully I would honorably keel over of a heart attack while singing a solo in church. At the very least, I hoped to actualize the Scripture's encouragement: "Beloved, do not think it strange concerning the fiery trial testing you; ...but rejoice to the extent that you partake of Christ's sufferings, that when His glory is revealed, you may also be glad with exceeding joy."[108] Eventually however, I could not sustain any affection for suffering, because wonder of wonders, it hurt too much. How was it that my attempts to participate in Christ's sufferings never resulted in the promised joy? Whatever my Pentecostal brethren taught me about suffering or however wrongly I interpreted their teaching, the result was I missed a vital message. Perhaps only in middle age have I been ready to hear it.

The message is this. *The cross of Christ generates the infinitely potent, therapeutic remedy for all suffering, sin, and death.* Orthodox theologian P. Evdokimov explains Jesus' parable from this remedial viewpoint, "Jesus the Savior…appears as the divine Healer… The therapeutic meaning of salvation…is the healing of a being and the elimination of the seed of mortality."[109] Evdokimov goes on to write,

> The extent of evil can be measured by the power of its antidote. The sick are healed by a treatment that befits the stature of God. The physician, *instead of the patient,* passes through death and inaugurates his universal healing: "Unless the grain of wheat falls into the earth and dies, it remains alone. But if it dies, it bears much fruit'…The *cross is planted at the threshold of the new life.*[110]

Thus, the parable puts the focus first on *Jesus* as the seed, bringing life to me a sinner. Only secondarily does Jesus use the parable to include my involvement with him. I am to interiorize Jesus' self-denial—or to use his hyperbolic expression—hate my life in this world, to help me return to the spiritual health God always desired for me. As a young person, I was right to suppose that suffering could signify solidarity with Christ—it is a truth experienced by countless believers through the ages. Furthermore, the Assemblies of God's stress on holiness still properly forms part of the bedrock of my faith.

My mistake lay in setting the conditions of my personal devotion and emotional experience (whether suffering or ecstasy) as the measure of Christ's potency. His cross—not my anxious piety—is planted at the threshold of my life. It is the tree God planted, as St. John the Revelator wrote, for the healing of the nations, and that includes restoration for my little realm.[111]

I have yet to incorporate thoroughly what this entails. Some mornings I awake in trepidation that circumstances will tip me into an abyss of affliction. The enemy whispers, "There is no resurrection, there is no joy, there is only suffering." Where once I fought this demon virtually alone, reading my Bible, and desperately praying for encouragement, the Orthodox Church routinely picks up the slack in my faith.

Hearing my morbid browbeating, my father confessor assigns me the "penance" to laugh more and stop taking myself so seriously. Each Mass I enter the parish and hear the opening Psalm: "Why go I so heavily while the enemy oppresseth me? O, send out thy light and thy truth… that I may go unto the altar of God, even the God of my *joy*." Each year on Good Friday, at the apex of cosmic suffering, the Church announces, "By the cross *joy* has come into the world."

Accordingly, Christ's therapeutic salvation charts the course of my journey.[112] Yes, Jesus calls me to bear my trials and grapple with my inadequacies, in essence, to pick up my own cross, but I sail to a glorious destiny under the flag of *his* cross. Since Christ's cross heals all suffering, the Church urges me to relinquish my obsessive "attachment to sorrow and agonizing sensitivity," and invite in joy.[113]

That God has granted me the gift of a husband with a quirky sense of humor does not hurt either.

Lynette A. Smith

# Living Out My Baptism

One Sunday, a diminutive eight-year-old let go of her mother's hand and cautiously descended into the church baptistery. She felt her heart thud under the ballooning white robe and reached out for her pastor-father's steadying hands. As she stood in water nearly to her neck, she affirmed her faith in Christ and added a personal declaration, "I'm glad I'm saved." Then her father immersed her in the name of the Father, Son, and Holy Spirit. To this day, the girl recalls the chuckle floating from where her mother awaited to help dry her and change her clothes. When she asked her mom why she had laughed at her, the mother said she was happy for her, that's all.

What a warm memory. I was pleased to learn at catechism classes prior to joining the Orthodox Church that I did not have to disregard my childhood water baptism and be "rebaptized" as some groups do with converts from other denominations. Since I was baptized in the name of the Trinity, the economy of God provided whatever might have been originally omitted. In a manner of speaking, my baptism was a done deal—"I'm glad I am saved"—but only in a manner of speaking. "Live out your baptism," the catechism directs me. Baptism extends far beyond obeying an ordinance, something I do because Jesus commanded it. It is even more than a declaration of faith. St. Paul describes the essence of baptism and its application to my life:

> We were buried with Him through baptism into death, that just as Christ was raised from the dead by the glory of the Father, even so we also should

walk in newness of life. For if we have been planted together in the likeness of his death, certainly we also shall be planted in his resurrection. Knowing this, that our old self was crucified with Him, that the body of sin might be done away with, that we should no longer be slaves of sin... Therefore do not let sin reign in your mortal body, that you should obey it in its strong impulses.[114]

Referring to this Scripture, St. John Chrysostom comments that I experience two deaths: one Christ has done already, and the other death is my job to work on after baptism.[115] I experience the first death only through Christ's vicarious act, because I can never destroy death, sin, and hell through my own oblation; I can never save myself, nor am I supposed to try. What a relief.

St. Cyril of Jerusalem catches me up in his enthusiasm for this holy Mystery:

> O strange and inconceivable thing! We did not really die, we were not really buried, we were not really crucified and raised again; but our imitation was in a figure, and our salvation in reality. Christ was actually crucified, and actually buried, and truly rose again; and all these things He has freely bestowed upon us, that we, sharing His sufferings by imitation, might gain salvation in reality.[116]

Orthodoxy teaches that in baptism God restores my fallen nature and imparts his power to obliterate my former transgressions. Baptism also protects against future habitual sins; however, the protection works in tandem with my effort to die to sin. This second death to which Chrysostom refers means that I change my focus from sin to holiness. The Holy Spirit within me provides the larger end of the strength I need, but I hold the responsibility to cooperate with him. On the one hand, such Orthodox teaching draws me away from extreme doctrines about salvation. I neither single-handedly will myself into holiness, nor lay passively depraved with no will of my own to change. On the other hand, Orthodoxy declares that baptism invokes an extreme measure of combat: I declare war on everything that is against God.[117]

Having lived several decades fighting recurrent types of sin, I could name my battle the Forty-Years War. Deep in the middle of combat with an aggressive sin such as judgmentalism, I weary to the point of almost believing it will take me captive. Chrysostom, however, does not buy into my slave mentality. In response to Paul's words, "Do not let sin reign in your mortal body," he says, "[Christ] came not to destroy our nature, but to set our free choice aright...it is not through any force or necessity that we are held down by iniquity, but willingly...[118] In other words, because of my baptism, I possess the will and the freedom to "walk in newness of life." Chrysostom claims that as a citizen of God's kingdom my temptation to concede defeat is irrational.

> It is absurd for those who are being conducted to the kingdom of heaven to have sin act as an Empress over them...It is as though one should hurl the diadem from off his head, and choose to be the slave of a frantic woman, who came begging, and was clothed in rags.[119]

Chrysostom submits that I need a good dose of heroism and persistence in the face of constant struggle. He also understands that I dread having to fight sin for the balance of my earthly journey. He assures me although I carry "a heavy task to get the upper hand of sin" my struggles are temporary "and will bring themselves to a close" when I physically die. Is this true comfort, though? Is death not the greatest, gruesome battle in which decay defeats life?

In remembering my baptism, I realize I became a partaker in *all* Jesus' saving acts. When my father drew me up out of the water, I acknowledged that as God raised his Son, he will eventually raise my body, and give me life everlasting. My comfort in my struggle is this; God's promise gives me life.[120]

# Remember Me

At least once a week, I deliberately slip into the holy orb of *anamnesis*. I suspend focus on my individual sphere of life and join the priest and fellow celebrants in our temple to remember Christ and his death. To Orthodox, the Greek word for remembrance, *anamnesis,* possesses a characteristic beyond the English meaning, "to call to mind an event or person." It also signifies that we experience a living reality of whom and what we remember. The event is not just in the past, but we somehow also actualize it today.

Within the realm of liturgical anamnesis, our remembrance encompasses far more than to recall the Last Supper, Jesus' passion, death, resurrection, and ascension. We bring the work and presence of Jesus into our midst.[121] "The liturgical mystery goes beyond simple commemoration. It 're-presents' the event, even *becomes* the event."[122] Through partaking of the Eucharist, we mystically assimilate Jesus' real presence, his continual love and self-giving to us.

As we begin the process to consecrate the bread and wine, the priest draws us into the sphere of anamnesis.[123] He recites that Jesus instituted and "commanded us to continue a perpetual memory of his precious death and sacrifice, until his coming again." At this, bells ring. Something important is about to happen. "For in the night in which Jesus was betrayed, he took bread...likewise, he took the cup..." With each gift of bread and wine to his disciples, Jesus invites them to partake and requests, "Do this in remembrance of me." The priest responds to Christ's request with, "We offer unto thee (God), the memorial thy Son hath commanded us to make; having in remembrance his blessed passion and precious death, his mighty resurrection and glorious ascension." We twenty-first century Christians are also there in that Upper Room, ready to take into ourselves Jesus' gifts.

Then the priest asks that the Holy Spirit change the bread and wine into the Body and Blood of Jesus. He prays, "Grant that we, receiving them...in remembrance of his death and passion, may be partakers of his most blessed Body and Blood." Soon after, the priest states that not only are we offering the fruit of our earthly labor—bread and wine—but we offer "our selves, our souls and bodies, to be a reasonable, holy, and living sacrifice." He asks that all partakers of the communion be filled with God's grace and blessing, "made one body with him (Jesus), that he may dwell in us and we in him." Memory is about to become actualized.

When I make my way to the altar rail, the corporate preparation now becomes a highly personal experience: I eat, I imbibe, I internalize Christ. A prayer one may privately offer after Mass unabashedly mingles this physical and spiritual mystery:

> Soul of Christ, sanctify me.
> Body of Christ, save me.
> Blood of Christ, inebriate me.
> Water from the side of Christ, save me.
> Passion of Christ, strengthen me.
> O good Jesus, hear me.
> Within thy wounds hide me.[124]

Earlier, I described holy anamnesis as an orb; this is because the energy of remembrance revolves in a circle of reciprocity. As Jesus offers me his body and blood, so I offer him my soul and body. As Jesus asks that I remember him, so I ask him to remember me. We sing an ancient hymn during Communion that ends, "like the thief will I confess thee: remember me, O Lord, in thy Kingdom."[125] And in my heart, I hear Jesus' reply, "Today you shall be with me in paradise." Jesus' anamnesis, his remembrance of me brings me perpetually into his presence.

The act of reciprocal remembrance during Divine Liturgy strengthens my resolve to enact it after I leave the parish nave, to invoke a continuous openness to Christ's presence in my daily life. I renew my hope that he will increasingly activate his self-giving death and resurrection in me, so that I too become self-giving and ever more dwell in him.

Lynette A. Smith

# Over Everything

*And over all these virtues put on love, which binds them all together in perfect unity.*[126]

Paul the Apostle

People are supposed to dread turning fifty; women reputedly begin to fudge their age even earlier. Somehow I managed to arrive at the half-century with a positive, receptive attitude, and with unmerited favor, my husband, family, and friends spoiled me my entire birthday month. They poured out their love in word and deed until I was filled with so much happiness and gratitude, a kind of lightness and energy infused my mind and body. I felt empowered; with these loved ones in my corner I could do anything, overcome any obstacle. Even as the air of my pleasure balloon gradually seeped out, and my feet touched the ground once more, I believed I had experienced a small epiphany. To the degree that I am open to true unadulterated love, given freely, that love transforms me in some way.

Of all the commendable qualities the Church reports of certain saints, the most astounding is their depth of love. Some spiritual directors of more recent times hold this reputation, such as St. Seraphim of Sarov, Father Arseny (mentioned earlier), and Maximos of Cyprus (featured in Markides' *The Mountain of Silence* and *Gifts of the Desert.*) Paul Evdokimov suggests that these souls have died to the world and unconditionally cast themselves on God and his mercy. They have been so purified and filled with the love of God that they turn the passions toward one supreme care for everyone. They possess "a heart aflame with love for the entire creation, for people, birds, beasts, evil spirits, all creatures." They "condemn neither sinners nor the children of this age…Such a one desires to love and venerate all without any distinction."[127] This level of love often effects radical change in its recipients, who may be moved to a greater, conscious yearning for God in spite of themselves.

I drink in the stories of these supreme Lovers, longing not only to meet such people, but also to evolve into this kind of lover myself. I wish I were daring enough to dive unreservedly into the abyss of God's love. I envision my insular life freed to embrace the whole groaning, broken world, to hope untiringly for its repentance and restoration. Convinced each person bears the image of God, however minuscule and shadowed it might be, I would shine Christ's light on my exhausted grocery checker, a rude church deacon, a deranged pan-handler, an insolent teenager, or my greedy boss. What wild things might happen if I regarded everyone I met as "my Joy" as St. Seraphim did?

Of course, even a superficial examination of my day-to-day motives and actions reveals a large fissure in the strength of my commitment to love so fully. The challenge remains to close that gap, a prospect that at once attracts my soul and devastates my ego. What unconditional love requires is for the ego to relinquish all inner barriers and resistances to God's love. To move in this direction, Orthodox tradition encourages each holy lover and would-be lover to follow the "Threefold Way" path of spiritual development. First, *catharsis*, purification of the soul from egotistical passions; second, *fotisis*, enlightenment of the soul through the Holy Spirit, and finally, *theosis*, ultimate union with God in total love.[128]

From all evidence, most of my journey is comprised of cathartic fits and starts to purify myself. However, if I focus too much on cleaning up my act and neglect to replace vices with virtues, I set up a security risk. I may strip my inner altar of its idols, but I should not then leave it bare of fotisis, enlightenment. Jesus warned that he can exorcise the evil from my heart, and I can proceed to "sweep the house clean" of sin, but if I do not then invite his Holy Spirit to occupy my life and fill it with love, evil will return with a vengeance.[129]

St. Paul offers his own slant on embracing the journey of spiritual development toward the ultimate life of love. He tells the Colossians:

> Put on the new nature, which is renewed in knowledge in the image of its Creator...Put on tender mercies, kindness, humility, meekness, longsuffering; bearing with one another, and forgiving one another, if anyone has a complaint against another; even as Christ forgave you, so you also must do. But over everything put on love, which is the bond of perfection."[130]

St. Chrysostom comments on why Paul highlights love above the other qualities.

> It is possible for one to be kind, and meek and humble minded, longsuffering, and yet not affectionate...all those things disintegrate, except they are done with love. Love is what clenches them all together. Whatever good thing you can list, if love is absent, it is nothing; it melts away..."[131]

There is then one chief reason I bother to engage in catharsis and crucify the old, rotting falsity of sin. It is to live in the genuine self that is being renewed in Christ's image. He embodies love, and this is the godlike quality he means me to develop. I was born for love. So I press on to keep to the "Threefold Path" of my journey, praying that however many of the next fifty years God lets me live on earth, over everything I will learn to put on love.

# It's to Die For

I'm just dying to eat a chocolate, dying to swig an Evian. I'm just dying for a smoke, dying to knock back a beer. I'm just dying to buy those shoes, dying to show them off. I'm just dying to meet Meryl Streep, dying to hear Eric Clapton. I'm just dying to get some sleep, dying to sleep with you. I'm just dying to find a partner, dying to take out my rival. I'm just dying to have a kid, dying to pack him off to school. I'm just dying for a promotion, dying to take a break. I'm just dying to go on vacation, dying to get back home.

I'm just living to die.

I'm just dying to eat the Bread, dying to plunge in Living Water. I'm just dying to inhale Divine Breath, dying to drink the Wine. I'm just dying to stride the skies, dying to share the glory. I'm just dying to meet the Morningstar, dying to hear Gabriel. I'm just dying to laugh away the nightmare, dying to sleep in Paradise. I'm just dying to esteem my spouse over myself, dying to forgive my enemy. I'm just dying to be fertile with vision, dying to blaze in wisdom. I'm just dying to shed my dragon skin, dying to break these chains. I'm just dying to leave my phantom self, dying to enter the Kingdom.

I'm just dying to live.

Lynette A. Smith

# ARE WE THERE YET?

To reach its final destination, a ship must have a navigational map that the captain uses along with a sextant or GPS to stay on course. At any given time, he knows where the ship is in the vast ocean. Years of experience combined with tools enable him to chart an accurate schedule for arrival, and the passengers plan their trip accordingly. In the Christian voyage aboard the Church, we know something of our destination—the Kingdom of heaven—but only the captain, Christ, knows when we will arrive and what kingdom life will actually be like for us.[132]

In my personal spiritual progress, it is both humbling and liberating for me to accept I possess a very limited ability to evaluate it. Eventually I will come into full communion with Christ, but I do not know exactly where I am in that process today. Furthermore, I might understand that after I die, I will go to meet Christ in Paradise, but I do not know the hour of my death. Only God knows, and wisely, he is not telling. My voyage requires faith in his gracious leadership. In the meantime, because the journey is arduous and fraught with myriad challenges, I am learning how to rest in the now and enjoy the beauty that surrounds me. I also need to receive the encouragement of those who have already arrived at our destination and cheer me on until the journey is complete.

Lynette A. Smith

# Tracking Spiritual Progress

In 1984, I lived on a Bible School campus in the northern highlands of Sulawesi, Indonesia for almost six months, attempting to help missionaries with projects. A single missionary woman, Tanja,* and I became friends, and we decided to take a four-day vacation on the small island of Saladin near Manado, the capital city. We hired a dual outrigger canoe, whose captain took us to a prime snorkeling spot before dropping us off at the island. I knew the marine life would be beautiful, although I did not learn until later that to put my facemask into the Sulawesi Sea was to feast my eyes on one of the world's richest levels of biodiversity.[133]

Prior to this trip, Tanja, an expert swimmer, had taught me how to snorkel in shallow coral reefs near shore, so I had a false sense that I could snorkel anywhere. One problem though, I could float but was no swimmer and had no clue how to tread water in depths over my head. In my pride, I did not make Tanja aware of this. If I had known what I know now—that the Sulawesi Sea is extremely deep, some 20,000 feet at its maximum—I would have had the good sense to put my feet up on the bow and snooze while Tanja explored. By the time the captain cut the engine over the diving area, I was a rigid body of determination and terror. Tanja slipped off the boat into the water and began calmly sightseeing.

I too climbed off, believing against all hope I could maintain a floating position with the aid of my life vest and fins. To my shock and horror, the waves hit me with a force that immediately drew me under their power, and

---

* Not her real name.

my snorkel took in water. It felt like the saline solution of death. I kicked and fought to right myself and grab the boat's beam, while the captain called Tanja to swim over to help him haul me back into the boat. I gradually recovered, shivering in spite of the equatorial sun. At her probing, I confessed my distorted reasoning, and she gently scolded me for such foolhardiness. The captain shook his head in astonishment that anyone could be so naïve. I had become the embodiment of the idiom, "in over her head."

When she had sufficiently calmed me down, Tanja took me back into the water and taught me how to relax into the rolling waves. Then, she threaded her arm through mine, and we swam away from the boat. I was still uneasy, especially when we hovered above an impenetrably sheer cliff. Surely if I stared too long over its edge, the blackness would suck me into its everlasting abyss. Tanja never let go of me, however, and together we took in the most exotic, lovely world I will ever see in my lifetime. Eventually we returned safely back to the boat.

As I fell alarmingly short of assessing my ability to snorkel alone in the ocean, so left to my own devises, I miscalculate the limits of my spiritual capacity. Whether from pride, stupidity, or myopia, I can deceive myself into taking on more ascesis than necessary. I overextend my inner resources, and burn out, risking resentment and bitterness until in a kind of backlash I become reluctant to launch once more into deepening relationship with Christ.

I can also easily misjudge my level of spiritual perfection. Depending on the circumstances, my self-evaluation swings between despondency and vainglory. A few years ago, Hieromonk Damascene advised attendees at my diocese's Parish Life Conference:

> The Holy Fathers counsel us that we are not to try to measure our spiritual progress. [It] can lead to pride on the one hand, and to despair on the other. If we think, 'I'm making great progress, I'm becoming holy,' we can be sure that we are not making progress, because we are being prideful, and pride separates us from God. On the other hand, if we despair about what seems to be our lack of progress, this despair also separates us from God. So, let God do the measuring of our progress. [134]

Although God alone tracks my spiritual development, I benefit from taking an occasional inventory of both weaknesses and emerging strengths. Not just on my own, though. Most Orthodox books I have read on the spiritual life emphasize that I need a mature guide or father confessor. I received Tanja's expert help only when I confessed to her my fear and inexperience of the ocean. Likewise, I do not obtain objective spiritual assistance unless I humble myself and ask for it.

If an angel came down from heaven, revealed to me the holy navigational map of my faith, and asked me to mark my location, I could not show him, and I should not try. It is enough to know that by God's grace, my journey has begun well and will end well. This is as it should be. Damascene noted, "It is ours only to leave behind all that separates us from God, to turn to God with our whole being, and to let God do the rest."[135]

Lynette A. Smith

## As it was in the Beginning, Is Now . . .

Awhile back, my husband and I played a game of racquetball at the community recreation center. I had not wanted to go, but did for Dennis' sake and because the exercise was good for us. I felt sluggish and heavy. The longer I played, the angrier I became with my body. "So what's new?" I chided myself. "You've gotten lazy with exercising again; you don't stretch out every day; you've slacked off on walking. And what about those weights? No wonder you're not a ball of fire. You've sabotaged your energy and enjoyment for the game. Again. When are you ever going to buckle down and get into shape?"

My evaluation of personal spiritual fitness often suffers from a similar annoyance. After decades of training, shouldn't I be better at this already? I do take some comfort in discovering that other Christians also wonder. Even a genius of Christian theology, C.S. Lewis, bemoans this frustration:

> By now I should be entering on the supreme stage
> Of the whole walk, reserved for the late
>     afternoon.
> The heat was to be over now; the anxious
>     mountains,
> The airless valleys and the sun-baked rocks,
>     behind me...[136]

The upshot of it all is I chafe under taking the perpetual posture of a humble apprentice. How many years must it take to advance to being a gilded master of, say, patience? I have had to take my arrogance down a peg or two over the years since entering the Orthodox Church. My early exposure to the Divine Liturgy took me aback because of its constant call on God to have mercy and "forgive me a sinner." I interpreted this as the high-church version of a Jonathan Edwards type religion.[137] I wondered, "Do these people really think they have to start their Christian life all over with a 'sinner's prayer' every week? They must believe their salvation is constantly hanging by a thread." Since that initial shock to my theology, I have learned that the Orthodox understand salvation is more of a process than a status. I ask God's mercy continually because the cave of my heart is infinitely subterranean, my self-deception deep. I am saved, but I am also being saved, and I will go on being saved.

When the Western Rite parishes in my area initiated a Benedictine Oblate program, I discovered St. Benedict's Rule, which, although written for sixth century monastic life, contains aspects I can apply to my journey.[138] St. Benedict of Nursia (ca. 480 - ca. 547) incorporated the progressive understanding of salvation into his spirituality. He writes, "Whoever you are, therefore, who are hastening to the heavenly homeland, fulfill with the help of Christ this minimum Rule which we have written for beginners; and then at length under God's protection you will attain to the loftier heights of doctrine and virtue."[139] Modern day Benedictine Abbot Lawrence comments:

> We remain sinners all our lives and we are always just beginning the spiritual life. We learn some aspects of the spiritual life and we may be freed from certain sins. We shall still struggle . . . to be faithful to the Lord and we can always learn more of the spiritual life. This is an attitude that we

must root deeply in ourselves: we are always learning, we are always beginning.[140]

Toward the end of the second racquetball match, it dawned on me. Yes, I was suffering the consequences of my lack of action during the past several days, but I was also in the here and now. This minute, I *was* exercising. I could begin again, and leave yesterday's laziness behind. Enveloped within God's economy of timelessness, every moment is my genesis. It is the confession of faith I sing in the *Gloria Patri* woven throughout Orthodox services:

> Glory be to the Father, and to the Son, and to the Holy Spirit.
> As it was in the beginning, is now, and ever shall be, world without end. Amen.

Lynette A. Smith

# In Newness of Life

*Have mercy upon us, have mercy upon us, most merciful Father;*
*For Thy Son our Lord Jesus Christ's sake, forgive us all that is*
*past; and grant that we may ever hereafter serve and please Thee in*
*newness of life.*[141]

General Confession, Orthodox Missal

If I trouble to make resolutions at all, I customarily list
them out around the beginning of a New Year or my
birthday. Like most people, whether or not I keep to my
pledges is another issue. Resolutions are tough to fulfill
when I define their success or failure by whether or not I
kept to them for 365 days. This challenge is why I
appreciate the words of the above prayer we say during
every Divine Liturgy. The prayer helps me regularly reset
my determination to live a more godly life.

There are several powerful aspects to this prayer. It beats
Alcoholics Anonymous by at least four hundred years,
but contains the first seven of the group's Twelve Steps
in a nutshell.[142] First, we say the prayer as part of a general
confession to acknowledge and lament our sins. We do
not mince words. "We do earnestly repent, and are
heartily sorry for our misdoings; the remembrance of
them is grievous unto us, the burden of them is
intolerable."

Second, we request divine assistance, "have mercy." Too
often, I secretly judge the quality of my resolve by how
well I accomplished it myself, but if I really want to
become more fully human, as my Creator intends, I must
depend on His work of mercy in and for me through the
Lord Jesus Christ. Any idea that I am able to be an

"autonomous human being," is oxymoronic. Rather, the essence of my humanness consists of a synergistic relationship with God and others.[143]

Third, the prayer addresses the screw-ups of our past. The phrase, *forgive us all that is past*, is wide open. When I say it, I could be remembering the nasty little remark said to someone in the church foyer that morning. Or, I might be struggling with old family patterns of addiction and brokenness, started generations ago, that affect me now. The past is a huge, shadeless wilderness of possibility for beating my self up or for holding grudges. However, in this prayer, said week after week after week, I invoke the heavenly Father's forgiveness through Christ; for it is Christ's cross that is able to cast an infinitely wide and cooling shade over sin's glaring wasteland.

The prayer's fourth facet asks God for the opportunity to begin again, "...*grant that we may ever hereafter serve and please thee...*" A religious slogan has floated around America for a few decades: "God is a God of second chances." That is not exactly true. Jesus implicitly suggested that the Father is a God of "seventy times seven" chances.[144] That is, he gives as many opportunities for forgiveness and a fresh start as I will choose to take advantage. A fourth century hermit, Abba Poemen, reported that the mentor, Abba Prior, made a fresh beginning every single day."[145] The only real catch to God's provision is: will I avail myself of His mercy, or will I pull back? Being willing to take baby steps is one sure remedy for the diseases of perfectionism and pride. Taking baby steps does not mean I consign myself to stay an immature child for the rest of my life. Rather, I would like to envision myself a spiritual athlete who daily practices the plays until I get them down and become ready to win at game time.

We conclude our prayer with, "...*in newness of life, to the honor and glory of thy Name.*" The newness of each day that God grants me on earth points toward his gift of rejuvenation in my life. As I open myself to that potential, and take big or small steps into His gracious love, I will bring honor and delight to my Creator.

The prayer may be finished, but the therapeutic work I need done is not. Something that no confession said in solitude provides or that any AA's Twelve Steps include is a priest's verbal pronouncement of God's forgiveness and affirmation of God's continual support.

> Almighty God, our heavenly Father, who of his great mercy has promised forgiveness of sins to all those who with hearty repentance and true faith turn unto him, have mercy upon you, pardon and deliver you from all your sins, confirm and strengthen you in all goodness, and bring you to everlasting life; through Jesus Christ our Lord.

A popular self-improvement axiom touts that I should not wait for someone to give me permission to take action, and this is a valuable suggestion for taking personal initiative. However, at the secret root of my being, there is nothing more I would like to hear outside my own little brain than the voice of authority declaring God Almighty has forgiven my failures and validates our familial relationship. I need to hear again that God is the strength of my life and that the outcome of decisions and events do not completely hang on my shoulders. Further, only God can bring me to everlasting life. Such priestly affirmation brings needed restoration and sets up the conditions for me to keep going forward "in newness of life" to my destiny into the Kingdom of heaven.

# Come Aside and Rest

*Jesus said to his disciples, "Come aside by yourselves to a deserted place and rest a while." For there were many coming and going, and they did not even have time to eat.*[146]

Mark the Evangelist

Making ports of call is integral to extended ocean voyages, and taking opportunities to "dock" and rest from strenuous endeavor is an important part of my Christian journey. Curiously, desert monastics and the early Church Fathers speak very little about resting unless they are referring to the ultimate, eternal rest believers enjoy after death. They do discuss acquiring stillness, *hesychia*, and assert that people who practice *hesychasm* will consequently experience rest of heart and mind.

However, when these spiritual teachers talk about rest they are not usually encouraging their disciples to relax. To them, rest comes from actively learning to still one's thoughts and fill the mind with contemplation of God. This was strenuous and often painful work. Early ascetics taught themselves to still the mind not only through meditation, but also in physical privations and mortifications such as severe fasting, heavy manual labor, limited hours of sleep, or minimal clothing in any weather. They understood that pain can sharpen the soul's awareness of its need for God. After they struggled under these sorts of disciplines, in time they might experience a breakthrough to substantial rest in mind, body, and soul. That is, so long as they used these harsh methods only as a *means* to that end.

Ancient ascetical techniques to acquire spiritual rest are never going to work for me. Twenty-first century Christians are overworked and overstressed in ways early ascetics could not have imagined. Evdokimov, in his *Ages of the Spiritual Life*, observes, "Today the combat is not the same. We no longer need added pain. Hair shirts, chains and flagellation would risk uselessly breaking us."[147] Certainly, the era of desert spirituality played a vital role to champion utter passion for God, but genuine "Christian asceticism is only a method in the service of life, and it will seek to adapt itself to the new needs."[148]

Evdokimov suggests today's Christians use ascetical practices that help liberate us "from every kind of addiction—speed, noise, alcohol, and all kinds of stimulants."[149] Workplaces are hectic, face-paced, under staffed. We fill our family life with activities, sports, and church programs. We do not get enough sleep; we eat on the run and not necessarily the healthiest of foods. To recover from the strain, we overcompensate with hours in front of the TV, computer, or video game. Even vacations can be more trouble than they are worth; like turtles, we carry our responsibilities wherever we go. Ever changing technological gadgetry bombards our senses and tickles our fancies. Technology also enables us to know the conditions around most of the globe, and whether conscious of the strain or not, we bear collectively and internally the distress of a host of wars, natural disasters, ecological decimations, famine, disease, and oppression.

Contemporary ascesis, then, might be to train myself to stop certain activities to get adequate rest and sleep. It may be to set a discipline of bringing quiet into at least part of the day. Rather than watching TV or listening to the (often very negative) news, I can choose to do a hobby or talk with my spouse. Proper fasting may include cutting down on food consumption, over spending on superfluous items, and sharing with the disadvantaged. My ascesis may not look like someone else's because we all have different personalities, challenges, professions, and home lives. Clearly, however, whatever methods I use, my goal is the same as the old desert Ammas and Abbas: to find deep rest in the presence of God.

There is another kind of rest I find necessary to practice. Some of us—especially converts—are eager to gobble up as many books, podcasts, or blogs on Orthodox theology and spirituality as we can. We learn about the power of the Jesus Prayer, and dream that we can emulate the man in *The Way of the Pilgrim* who recited it thousands of times a day.[150] We try to make every service at the parish and volunteer for numerous worthy tasks. Then, one day, we realize we are exhausted. Our brains hurt, our fervor is spent; we do not care if we say another *Gloria Patri* again, and what is more, feel guilty that we don't care. I am one of those converts. A wise man of the Church, Metropolitan Anthony, understands this phenomenon. He warns that my overzealousness may be spiritual greed to have more of God than I am ready to assimilate, and that in trying to take on too much religious practice I suffer spiritual gluttony. Once the Metropolitan told a young lady who burnt herself out trying to pray for hours a day:

> You've got indigestion…There are moments when you can tell God, "I simply must rest. I have no strength to be with you all the time," which is perfectly true. You are still not capable of bearing God's company all the time. Well, say so. God knows that perfectly well, whatever you do

about it. Say... "I'll just have a rest. For a moment I accept to be less saintly."[151]

What did he suggest the lady do for rest? Go take in some beauty for a while. I think it is time I took his advice.

# Seen Any Beauty Lately?

In "Illustrators of the Holy Beautiful," I included several quotes from Orthodox teachers on beauty. I am discovering that the Church does not treat the subject as a peripheral item of interest—by the way, beauty is a god-thing. Rather, beauty is a vital catholic theology upheld from the time of the early Church Fathers such as Gregory of Nyssa, Maximus the Confessor, Gregory of Nazianzus, and Basil; to Gregory Palamas and John of the Cross in the Middle Ages. A well-honored and often referenced anthology of Eastern piety and asceticism, compiled in the late eighteenth century is entitled, the *Philokalia*, or love of the beautiful. More recently, Orthodox theologian, Paul Evdokimov, wrote a treatise on beauty as it pertains to art and religious iconography in particular.[152] At the heart of all their discussions on beauty stands the perfection and beauty of Christ, and that living in Christ beautifies me.

When I was about seventeen, I realized during my walk one day what an extraordinary blessing it was to notice nature. My senses and heart were wide open to nuances of light and shadow on the desert mesas, to details of color in stone, and the gentle scent of wild geraniums. For sustained moments, I could forget my griefs and enjoy the reality of God's manifested beauty. With all the fervor of teenage idealism, that day I promised myself to keep this awareness of beauty "always." For many years, I held onto that vow. Unfortunately, the longer I have lived, especially in Denver's growing metropolis, the less I have been able to keep that promise.

During one Lenten season, I had an opportunity to make what would be a unique choice for me. I could give up chocolate, evening TV, or spy novels for forty days. Or, I could relinquish an over-occupation with issues that bothered me in favor of being on the watch for the beautiful. I chose the latter, and no, this was not an evasion; sticking to this choice was rather difficult, in fact. For some of us, it can become a habit—even an odd pleasure—to plow our little brain cells down into well-worn grooves of favorite problems. Over and over, I break up the same barren ground. By the time I become tired of plowing and replowing over this poor soil, I have little energy left to look up and notice

> the lilies of the field,
> the sparrows of the air,
> the mountain of the Lord.

With every occasion that I choose to ignore some splash of splendor in favor of focusing on the cares of this life, I increasingly lose my sensitivity to the beautiful. I forget to be grateful and neglect my awe of the Holy. Consequently, I have no idea how to "gaze upon the beauty of the Lord."[153] I have allowed the loveliness that is in a light beam or a Rublev icon to become as invisible as the unseen God.

However, his creative impulse moving around and through me is precisely one way God has chosen to distribute hints of his glory. Those glimmers of splendor may even occasionally show up when I look in the mirror or lift my face in worship. St. Gregory of Nyssa confirms this:

You alone are an icon of Eternal beauty, and if you look at Him, you will become what He is, imitating Him who shines within you, whose glory is reflected in your purity. Nothing in all creation can equal your grandeur. All the heavens can fit in the palm of God's hand...and though He is so great...you can wholly embrace Him. He dwells within you...He pervades your entire being...[154]

Did I break my habit of ignoring beauty during Lent? No, but from that starting point, I have hacked a good hole in it through which I could observe the exquisiteness of creation once again.

Lynette A. Smith

# Fan Club of Saints

St. Hilda of Whitby's icon hangs above the communion altar at my parish with several icons of Western Orthodox Saints: Benedict, Bede, Alban, the first Christian martyr in England, and others. For her time, St. Hilda (614-680 AD) was one of the most powerful women in England. She built and led a double monastery (a community of monks and nuns) from which came several church leaders. Kings and princes asked her advice, and they so well respected her that she presided over a key synod of bishops to settle differences between Celtic and Roman Christian liturgical practices. According to her biographer, Venerable Bede, right up to her death at age sixty-six after a seven-year fever, Hilda continued "to instruct the flock committed to her charge; for by her own example she admonished all persons to serve God...and always to return thanks to Him in adversity, or bodily infirmity."[155]

Woefully, I am not always inspired to hear the "legend," or hagiography, of a saint. So and so lived in such and such a time, lived and died doing remarkable exploits for the Kingdom of God. How nice, these people; they just dove right into whatever fray was brewing in their time. I don't. They tended to give everything away. I haven't. They guided, silenced, or infuriated rulers with their exhortations. I don't want to be anywhere near a politician. Saints were the ones who would have been on the front lines of Sudan, Sumatra, New Orleans, and Haiti relief efforts. I stay home, pray, send money and a few emergency kits. They took one look at the scripture, "Let us throw off every encumbrance and the sin that so easily entangles, and run the race set before us," literally stripped down to the sparest of gear, and took off on the

Christian journey like Kenyan Olympic runners. I am the slug sitting in the stands muttering, "Wow, look at them go." They willingly suffered illness, humiliation, torture, and death because of Christ. I can only hope that if I face martyrdom, I will not renege on my loyalty.

Why does the Church play up the Saints, anyway, plastering their likenesses on walls and ceilings of parish and cathedral? Just to make me feel inadequate compared to them? See what *you* should be like, Lynette, you failure, you. Oddly, the Saints' visible presence in iconography frequently has a more positive effect on me than do some of their legends.

Iconographers of Christ, the Blessed Virgin, and the Saints deliberately paint their subjects without an external source of light. I never see them cast a shadow, nor are they bathed in a beam of light. The light source emanates from within their bodies. The nimbus glows about their head signifying that God's Uncreated Light has transformed them inside out. The Saint has become God-realized, or what the Holy Fathers call, *transparent*.

How does it happen that the Saints emanate such transparency and fullness of the Holy Spirit? St. Basil the Great explains that transparency happens as people withdraw from the passions that have alienated their souls from a close relationship with God. They become "purified from the shame whose stain they took through sin, and come back again to their natural beauty, as it were cleaning the Royal Image and restoring its ancient form" and are better able to draw nearer to God's Spirit. Then, Basil says,

Just as when a sunbeam falls on bright and transparent bodies, they themselves become brilliant too, and shed forth a fresh brightness from themselves, so souls wherein the Spirit dwells, illuminated by the Spirit, themselves become spiritual, and send forth their grace to others.[156]

No doubt about it, I am not yet transparent—I still have a lot of withdrawing from the passions to do. What would you call me? Am I opaque, or as my non-politically correct Children's Church leaders taught me, "black with sin"? When a soul is opaque, it is impenetrable to God's Light, completely closed off and shut down to his love. We rightly judge that some opaque souls do exist, living exclusively on the dark side of evil. However, the Holy elders are likely to pick the term "translucent" to describe most people's state of being. We do permit God's Light to pass through although our sin obscures his Presence. We are more or less translucent depending on how much we live according to the light we are given.

In other words, I am a blurry Christian. What flecks of Christ you may see refracting from my words, attitudes, and behavior are a real enough, but my deficiencies distort the sharp lines of his holy humility and love. At times, my behavior may be so rough around the edges that neither you nor I can recognize that Jesus dwells in me somewhere.

The Church has always had a choice: she can excuse translucency as just the way we humans are, or she can expose it as damnable hypocrisy. As tempting as it would be to land on one side or the other, historically the Church's elders have chosen to do neither. Rather, as St.

Basil puts it, "Through His [the Holy Spirit] aid hearts are lifted up, the weak are held by the hand, and they who are advancing are brought to perfection."[157] Translucency in this life is a matter of quest toward ultimate transparency in the next life. It is a matter of persistent patience with myself and with others under the hand of a Father "whose property is always to have mercy," as the liturgy of St. Tikhon says.

Consequently, the Orthodox Church refuses to be iconoclastic and leave the walls of her temples barren of a central belief she holds so dear. God is constantly working to return us to our pristine state of grace and reaching beyond even this, to live in union with him. The Saints are examples of that belief made into an increasing reality; they are witnesses to my future. Instead of me sitting in the grandstand watching them go, the Saints are looking down from all sides of the parish, cheering me on. Dare I say it—they are my fan club. Their straight postures, lithe bodies, calm attentive eyes, and reposed lips seem to invite:

> "Come receive the Light; come into the Body of Christ. All of us contend together, we in our way, you in yours. We died and live on; you die to live also. Every time you choose hope over cynicism, truth over self-deception, confession over concealment, humility over pride, love over hate, you join the journey into the Kingdom. One day you too will radiate with transparent glory and touch the face of the Son."

Thus, I continue my messy and glorious voyage toward the ultimate destiny God already prepared for humanity from the foundation of the world. By his great mercy and the prayers of the Saints, I shall arrive to share complete and unreserved communion with Father, Son, and Holy Spirit.

# NOTES

[1] Matt. 7:7; 13-14. Author's translation.

[2] Anthony M. Coniaris, *Philokalia: The Bible of Orthodox Spirituality*, (Minneapolis: Light and Life, 1998), 136.

[3] 1 Cor. 3:21-22.

[4] Ps. 77:19 (76:20 Septuagint).

[5] Exod. 14:8-16.

[6] C.f., Ps. 78.15

[7] C.f., Gen. 1:26-27; Eph. 1:4; 3:19; 1 Thess. 4:3a; Matt. 5:48.

[8] Gen. 3:1-7; Rom. 1:20-25.

[9] 2 Pet. 1:3-4; 1 John 3:2; 4:17.

[10] Eph. 1:11-12; Col. 2:9-10.

[11] John 17:20-26. C.f., John 15.

[12] Exod. 15:19-21.

[13] *The Anglican Breviary*, (Long Island, Frank Gavin Liturgical Foundation, Inc.: 1955; reprint, Chicago: R.R. Donnelley & Sons, Lakeside Press, 1998), 1097.

[14] C.f., Luke 2:25-32.This feast day is also known as the Circumcision of our Lord, or the Holy Family.

[15] *Anglican Breviary*, 1097.

[16] C.f., Hebrews 1:3.

[17] *Anglican Breviary*, 1099.

[18] Bernard Meehan, *The Book of Kells, An Illustrated Introduction to the Manuscript in Trinity College Dublin*, (London: Thames & Hudson Ltd, 1994).

[19] Ibid, 9.

[20] John Breck, "Divine Beauty (2)," *Life in Christ Series*. http://www.oca.org/CHRIST-life-article.asp?SID=6&ID=171.

[21] Coniaris, *Philokalia*, 12. C.f., Exod. 34:29-30; 35; 2 Cor. 3:12-18.

[22] Vladimir Berzonsky, "The Cloud of Unknowing," *Reflections in Christ Series*, http://www.oca.org/CHRIST-thoughts-print.asp?ID=348. Emphasis mine.

[23] Ibid.

[24] Ps. 96:9 (95:9 Septuagint).

[25] Ps. 27:4 (26:4 Septuagint).

[26] Luke 17:20-21.

[27] Matt. 13:45-46.

[28] Ephraim the Syrian "Hymn I," *Pearl*.

[29] Metropolitan PHILIP (Saliba) and Fr. Joseph J. Allen, *Out of the Depths Have I Cried: Thoughts on Incarnational Theology in the Eastern Orthodox Experience*, (Brookline, Mass: Holy Cross Orthodox Press, 1979), 13.

[30] Phil. 3:14.

[31] Luke 17:21.

[32] Walker Percy, *Lost in the Cosmos, The Last Self-Help Book*, (New York: Farrar, Straus, 1983).

[33] Coniaris, *Philokalia*, 253.

[34] Ibid., 251, 255.

[35] Rom. 2:15; 2 Cor. 10:4-5.

[36] John Climacus, *The Ladder of Divine Ascent,* Classics of Western Spirituality, trans. Colm Luibheid, Norman Russell, (Mahwah, NJ: Paulist Press, 1982), 240. References are from the Septuagint. In the NKJ they are Ps. 70:1;119:42;51.

[37] Phil. 4:6.

[38] John Cassian, *The Conferences,* trans. Boniface Ramsey, Ancient Christian Writers No. 57, (New York; Mahwah, N.J.: Newman Press, 1997), 57. Emphasis mine. C.f., Phil. 4:8.

[39] Theophan the Recluse, *The Spiritual Life, and How to be Attuned to It,* trans. Alexandra Dockham; 3rd printing, (Platina, Calif: St. Herman of Alaska Brotherhood, 2000), 257.

[40] Cassian, *Conferences,* 57.

[41] Climacus, *Ladder,* 240.

[42] Coniaris, *Philokalia,* 91.

[43] Philip Lawrence, "Prologue," *Study the Rule of St. Benedict,* http://christdesert.org/Detailed/63.html

[44] Coniaris, *Philokalia,* 77.

[45] Matt. 18:3-4 (New International Version).

[46] 3 John 1:9-10 (New International Version).

[47] Col. 3:16.

[48] Matt. 17:20.

[49] John Haslett, "Trapped in The Gyre," *Adventure* (Dec. 06/Jan. 07), 44.

[50] Ibid., 47.

[51] The Servant of God Alexander, *Father Arseny, 1893-1973: Priest, Prisoner, Spiritual Father*, trans. Vera Bouteneff, (Crestwood, NY: St. Vladimir's Seminary Press, 2000).

[52] *Father Arseny*, 44, 45.

[53] Luke 1:78-79 (King James Version).

[54] The story is from 2 Kings 6:8-17 (New International Version).

[55] Heb. 1:14.

[56] *Orthodox Missal: According to the Use of the Western Rite Vicariate of the Antiochian Orthodox Christian Archdiocese of North America*, (Stanton, N.J.: Saint Luke's Priory Press, 1995), 71.

[57] Num. 22:21-35.

[58] Eph. 4:18-19 (Author's adaptation).

[59] *Orthodox Missal*, 186.

[60] John 17:21, 24.

[61] Antiochian Orthodox Church, "Communion of Saints," in *What Orthodox Christians Believe*. Pamphlet.

[62] Ibid., "Prayer to the Saints." Pamphlet.

[63] *Anglican Breviary*, 1247.

[64] Ephraim creatively writes "a multitude of hymns to be chanted by choirs of women, which set forth the true doctrines, refuted heretical error, and praised the contests of the Martyrs." http://goarch.org/chapel/saints/406.

[65] http://www.catholic.org/saints/saint.php?saint_id=3.

[66] The Eastern Rite of the Church honors Ephraim on January 28, the Western Rite on June 18, and the Roman Catholic Church on June 9. No one is quite sure on which date he died, so he is celebrated three times a year.

[67] Original Nature: the pristine, luminous nature God originally created for Adam and Eve prior to their fall. This nature is made in the image and likeness of God.

[68] Metropolitan Anthony (Bloom) of Sourozh, *Living Prayer* (Springfield, Ill.: Templegate, 1966), viii.

[69] Ibid.

[70] Saliba and Allen, *Depths*, 78.

[71] Ibid., 85.

[72] Isa. 35:1 (New International Version.)

[73] Cassian, *Conferences*, 19.10.1.

[74] Matt. 4:1.

[75] Laura Swan, *The Forgotten Desert Mothers, Sayings, Lives, and Stories of Early Christian Women* (Mahwah, N.J.: Paulist Press, 2001), 65.

[76] Saliba and Allen, *Depths*, 71, 73.

[77] F. V. Joannes and Kazuyoshi Nomachi, *Sinai*, (New York: Everest House, 1978), 9.

[78] 2 Kings 2:11.

[79] Matt. 17:1-13.

[80] Mal. 4:5-6.

[81] Read the whole story in 1 Kings 18:20-19:19.

---

[82] Ps. 102:2,3,6 (101:3,4,7 Septuagint).

[83] 1 Pet. 3:4-6.

[84] Heb. 11:11.

[85] Philip Simmons, *Learning to Fall: The Blessings of an Imperfect Life*, (New York: Bantam Books, 2000), ix. Simmons, struck with Lou Gehrig's disease, writes about living through loss.

[86] 2 Pet. 3:4.

[87] Excerpts taken from Psa. 74 New International Version, (Ps. 73 Septuagint).

[88] Rom. 8:19-23; 2 Pet. 3:8-13; Apoc. 21:3-5.

[89] Matt. 11:28-30.

[90] John 12:24-26.

[91] John 15:5.

[92] Matt. 16:24-26//Luke 9:23-25//John 12:25-26.

[93] James 1:21.

[94] 1 Peter 1:6-7.

[95] 1 John 3:14;16.

[96] Gal. 2:20.

[97] Rom. 8:13; Col. 3:5.

[98] Col. 3:5-14; Eph. 4:22-24.

[99] 1 Cor. 9:26-27.

[100] Phil. 3:8-14; 1 Cor. 9:24-25.

[101] Heb. 12:1.

[102] Heb. 12:2.

[103] Gregory of Nazianzus *Oration* 43.7. In *Early Church Fathers.*

[104] John Chrysostom *John* 83.5. In *Early Church Fathers.*

[105] Jerome *Letter to Furia* 54.6. In *Early Church Fathers.*

[106] http://www.helpingyouharmonise.com/?q=metaphors

[107] John 12:24-25.

[108] 1 Peter 4:12-13.

[109] Paul Evdokimov, *Ages of the Spiritual Life,* trans. Sister Gertrude, revised trans. Michael Plekon and Alexis Vinogradov, (Crestwood, NY: St. Vladimir's Seminary Press, 1998), 184.

[110] Evdokimov, *Ages,* 184-5. Emphasis mine.

[111] Apoc. 22:2.

[112] Evdokimov, *Ages,* 185.

[113] Ibid.

[114] Romans 6:4-6, 12. Translation borrowed from J. B. Morris in St. John Chrysostom's *Epistle to the Romans*, Homily 11.

[115] John Chrysostom *Epistle to the Romans* 11.

[116] Cyril of Jerusalem *Catechetical Lectures* 20.5.

[117] Coniaris, *Philokalia,* 128. See also Evdokimov, *Ages,* 72.

[118] Chrysostom *Romans* 11.

[119] Ibid.

[120] C.f., Ps. 119:50 (118:50 Septuagint).

[121] Michael D. Keiser, *Offering the Lamb: Reflections on the Western Rite Mass in the Orthodox Church*, (Bloomington, Ind.: AuthorHouse, 2006), 62.

[122] Evdokimov, *Ages,* 241. Emphasis mine.

[123] *Orthodox Missal,* 185-186.

[124] *Anima Christi,* an early fourteenth century Roman Catholic prayer.

[125] *Of Thy Mystical Supper,* an ancient Byzantine hymn.

[126] Col. 3:14.

[127] Evdokimov, *Ages,* 195.

[128] Kyriacos C. Markides, *The Mountain of Silence,* (New York: Image Press, 2002), 213.

[129] Luke 11:24-26.

[130] Col. 3:8-13. Author's adaptation.

[131] Chrysostom, *Homilies on Colossians* 8. Emphasis mine.

[132] Scripture calls the present era "the last days," without specifying how many "days" will lapse before the end of time. C.f., Matt. 24:35-36.

[133] Bunaken National Park. http://www.north-sulawesi.org/bunaken.html.

[134] Hiermonk Damascene, *The Orthodox Word*, Vol. 41, (May-Aug, 2005), 147-168. From a talk given at the Parish Life Conference of the Antiochian Orthodox Diocese of Wichita and Mid-America, Sioux City, Iowa, June 9, 2005.

[135] Ibid.

---

[136] C.S. Lewis, *Poems*, "Pilgrim's Problem," ed. Walter Hooper, (San Diego, New York, London: Harcourt Brace Javanovich, 1964), 119.

[137] Jonathan Edwards was an American theologian in the 1700s, who in his famous sermon, "Sinners in the Hands of an Angry God," preached, "O sinner! Consider the fearful danger you are in: it is a great furnace of wrath, a wide and bottomless pit, full of the fire of wrath, that you are held over in the hand of that God, whose wrath is provoked and incensed as much against you, as against many of the damned in hell. You hang by a slender thread, with the flames of divine wrath flashing about it, and ready every moment to singe it, and burn it asunder."
http://www.ccel.org/ccel/edwards/sermons.sinners.html.

[138] The Benedict Fellowship of St. Lawrence, http://saintlaurenceosb.org/.

[139] The Rule of St. Benedict, *Chapter 73*.

[140] Lawrence, "Prologue," *Rule,* http://christdesert.org/Detailed/62.html.

[141] *Orthodox Missal,* 182.

[142] From *The Twelve Steps of Alcoholics Anonymous*. http://www.aa.org/en_pdfs/smf-121_en.pdf.

> 1. We admitted we were powerless over alcohol—that our lives had become unmanageable.
> 2. Came to believe that a Power greater than ourselves could restore us to sanity.
> 3. Made a decision to turn our will and our lives over to the care of God as we understood Him.
> 4. Made a searching and fearless moral inventory of ourselves.
> 5. Admitted to God, to ourselves, and to another human being the exact nature of our wrongs.
> 6. Were entirely ready to have God remove all these defects of character.
> 7. Humbly asked Him to remove our shortcomings.

[143] The Christian doctrine that the human will cooperates with the Holy Ghost in the work of renewal.

[144] Matt. 18:21-22.

[145] Yushi Nomura, *Desert Wisdom: Sayings from the Desert Fathers*, (Garden City, N.Y.: Doubleday & Co., Inc. 1982), 1.

[146] Mark 6:31

[147] Evdokimov, *Ages,* p. 64.

[148] Ibid.

[149] Ibid.

[150] Anonymous, *The Way of a Pilgrim, and The Pilgrim Continues His Way,* trans. Helen Bacovcin, (Garden City, N.Y., Image Books, a division of Doubleday and Co., Inc., 1978).

[151] Anthony Bloom, *Beginning to Pray,* (Mahwah, N.J.: Paulist Press, 1970), 77.

[152] Paul Evdokimov, *The Art of the Icon: A Theology of Beauty*, out of print (Oakwood Publications, 1989).

[153] Ps. 27:4 (26 Septuaguint).

[154] Coniaris, *Philokalia,* 17.

[155] Venerable Bede, *The Ecclesiastical History of the English People*, trans. Leo Sherley-Price, rev. ed., (New York: Penguin Classics, 1991).

[156] Basil the Great, *Holy Spirit* 9.23.

[157] Ibid.

Lynette A. Smith

---

# RECOMMENDED READING

Alexander, the Servant of God. *Father Arseny, 1893-1973: Priest, Prisoner, Spiritual Father*, trans. Vera Bouteneff, Crestwood, NY: St. Vladimir's Seminary Press, 2000.

Ante-Nicene, Nicene, Post-Nicene Fathers, 38 Vols.

Bloom, Metropolitan Anthony of Sourozh, *Living Prayer*, Springfield, Ill.: Templegate, 1966.

——————————————————————, *Beginning to Pray*, Mahwah, N.J.: Paulist Press, 1970.

Saint Climacus, John, *The Ladder of Divine Ascent,* Classics of Western Spirituality, trans., Colm Luibheid, Norman Russell, Mahwah, N.J.: Paulist Press, 1982.

Coniaris, Fr. Anthony M., *Philokalia: The Bible of Orthodox Spirituality,* Minneapolis: Light and Life, 1998.

Evdokimov, Paul, *Ages of the Spiritual Life,* trans. Sister Gertrude, rev. trans., Michael Plekon and Alexis Vinogradov, Crestwood, NY: St. Vladimir's Seminary Press, 1998.

Keiser, Fr. Michael D., *Offering the Lamb: Reflections on the Western Rite Mass in the Orthodox Church,* Bloomington, Ind.: AuthorHouse, 2006.

Lawrence, Abbot Philip, *Study the Rule of St. Benedict,*
  http://christdesert.org/.

Markides, Kyriacos C., *The Mountain of Silence,* New York:
  Image Press, 2002.

Meehan, Bernard. *The Book of Kells, An Illustrated
  Introduction to the Manuscript in Trinity College Dublin,*
  London: Thames & Hudson Ltd, 1994.

Nomura, Yushi. *Desert Wisdom: Sayings from the Desert
  Fathers,* Garden City, N.Y.: Doubleday & Co., Inc.
  1982.

Saliba, Metropolitan Philip, and Allen, Fr. Joseph J., *Out of
  the Depths Have I Cried: Thoughts on Incarnational
  Theology in the Eastern Orthodox Experience,*
  Brookline, Mass.: Holy Cross Orthodox Press,
  1979.

Schmemman, Fr. Alexander, *For the Life of the World,*
  Crestwood, N.Y.: St. Vladimir's Seminary Press,
  1972.

Saint Theophan the Recluse, *The Spiritual Life, and How to
  be Attuned to It,* trans. Alexandra Dockham,
  Platina, Calif: St. Herman of Alaska Brotherhood,
  2000.

Ware, Kallistos (Bishop), *The Power of the Name: The Jesus
  Prayer in Orthodox Spirituality,* Fairacres Oxford:
  SLG Press, Convent of the Incarnation: 1974,
  new ed.1986.